MACMILLAN MODERN DRAMATISTS

DATE DUE

APR 29 1995	

BRODART   Cat. No. 23-221

Macmillan Modern Dramatists
Series Editors: *Bruce King and Adele King*

Published titles

MACMILLAN MODERN DRAMATISTS

EDWARD ALBEE

Gerry McCarthy

Lecturer in Drama and Theatre Arts
University of Birmingham

MACMILLAN

First published 1987

Published by
Higher and Further Education Division
MACMILLAN PUBLISHERS LTD
Houndmills, Basingstoke, Hampshire RG21 2XS
and London
Companies and representatives
throughout the world

Typeset by
Wessex Typesetters
(Division of The Eastern Press Ltd)
Frome, Somerset

Printed in Hong Kong

British Library Cataloguing in Publication Data
McCarthy, Gerry
Edward Albee.—(Macmillan modern dramatists)
1. Albee, Edward—Criticism and interpretation
I. Title
812'.54   PS3551.L25Z/

ISBN 0–333–30119–6

For Moira

Contents

List of Plates

and Neil Fitzgerald (Martin Beck Theatre 1971). Photograph © Martha Swope.
7. Fred Voelpel's costumes for Albee's 1975 production of *Seascape* at the Sam S. Shubert Theatre, NYC. Photograph courtesy Billy Rose Theatre Collection.
8. Frances Conroy and Jo Musante in *The Lady from Dubuque* directed by Alan Schneider in 1980. Photograph © Martha Swope.

The author and publishers are grateful to copyright holders for permission to reproduce photographs.

Acknowledgements

The author and publishers would like to thank the following for permission to reproduce copyright material: Edward Albee and Atheneum for excerpts from *Who's Afraid of Virginia Woolf?*, copyright © 1962 Edward Albee; *A Delicate Balance*, copyright © 1966 Edward Albee; *All Over*, copyright © 1971 Edward Albee; *Seascape*, copyright © 1975 Edward Albee; *Listening*, copyright © 1975, 1977 Edward Albee; and *The Lady from Dubuque*, copyright © 1977, 1980 Edward Albee. Reproduced with the permission of Atheneum Publishers. Edward Albee and Jonathan Cape for permission to reproduce excerpts from *The Death of Bessie Smith*, *Zoo Story* and *The Sandbox*, all copyright © 1960 Edward Albee, and *Who's Afraid of Virginia Woolf*. The Putnam Publishing Group for excerpts from *The Sandbox*, *The Death of Besse Smith* and *Zoo Story* from *The Plays: Volume 1* by Edward Albee, copyright © 1981 Edward Albee. Alix Jeffry, the Harvard Theatre Collection, Martha Swope and the New York Public Library for permission to reproduce photographs from productions of Albee plays.

Editors' Preface

The *Macmillan Modern Dramatists* is an international series of introductions to major and significant nineteenth and twentieth-century dramatists, movements and new forms of drama in Europe, Great Britain, America and new nations such as Nigeria and Trinidad. Besides new studies of great and influential dramatists of the past, the series includes volumes on contemporary authors, recent trends in the theatre and on many dramatists, such as writers of farce, who have created theatre 'classics' while being neglected by literary criticism. The volumes in the series devoted to individual dramatists include a biography, a survey of the plays, and detailed analysis of the most significant plays, along with discussion, where relevant, of the political, social, historical and theatrical context. The authors of the volumes, who are involved with theatre as playwrights, directors, actors, teachers and critics, are concerned with the plays as theatre and discuss such matters as performance, character interpretation and staging, along with themes and contexts.

BRUCE KING
ADELE KING

1
Introduction

Edward Albee saw *The Zoo Story* first performed in German, a language he was unable to understand. By a series of chances the play which had been refused in New York was premiered in 1959 in Berlin, and Europe and saw the debut of the most significant American dramatist of his generation. New York was eager to celebrate the success of Albee and the new writers of the sixties, but at the same time provided a theatrical system which did little to promote their talents. Following a favourable reception in Berlin *The Zoo Story* was rapidly produced off-Broadway at the Cricket Theatre in a double bill with Samuel Beckett's *Krapp's Last Tape*.

It was the beginning of the years in which the marginal theatres of New York were to produce an extraordinary profusion of new writing and theatrical experimentation. Albee himself, with his European production behind him, was 'discovered' by the American public in one of the small theatres off Broadway, where there was an audience for the European avant-garde whose reputations were already established, and for a repertoire of classics and modern revivals. His work, however, corresponds with a wave of writing including the plays of Jack Richardson, Jack Gelber and Kenneth Brown, who were to be performed off-off-Broadway in the subsistence economy of the real experimental fringe. Here performance was a courageous enterprise carried on in lofts, cafés, church halls and basements; anywhere that a fit-up stage or performance space could be created. Concentrated in downtown Manhattan these 'theatres' constituted the heart of a veritable artistic community which triumphantly overturned conventional ideas of theatre as entertainment and as a social occasion. Ruby Cohn has described this as a theatre 'with no tradition but a rebellious spirit'.[1] Although Albee's career destined him to move from off-Broadway to take his chances in successively more and more perilous ventures on Broadway itself, his response to theatre has much in common with the best of the rebellion against the New York theatre establishment. He might well have fought his battles on the fringe, had it not been for his sudden and complete success.

The impact of *The Zoo Story* was reinforced by the performance of *The Death of Bessie Smith* (1960 – another Berlin premiere) and *The Sandbox*, commissioned by the Spoleto Festival, both performed the same year in New York. The press was generally rapturous, but Albee remained guarded. He announced two projects: *The American Dream*, a play from which the characters of *The Sandbox* had been taken, and a full-length play, for which he had two titles in mind: *The Exorcism*, or *Who's Afraid of Virginia Woolf?* These two plays were rapidly completed and performed in 1961 and 1962. In four years of writing and within two years of his New York debut, Albee had emerged as a dramatist second to none in the United

States. His works were beginning to appear in print, and his first full-length play was a smash hit on Broadway.

'Careers are mysterious things', Albee ruminated at the time, as he considered the enthusiasm with which his first plays were being received. The critics who hailed him as the virtual saviour of serious American theatre would be as immoderate in their blame as in their praise, when in later years there was no obvious successor to the play which confirmed his instant reputation: *Who's Afraid of Virginia Woolf?* (1962)

The extraordinary thing about this newcomer was the apparent lack of any apprenticeship. Albee came fully fledged as a playwright of international stature. In his first works there was a power of imagination, a versatility, and a sheer talent comparable for many with the pioneering genius of American theatre, Eugene O'Neill. From the outset comparisons abounded: he was the successor to Arthur Miller and Tennessee Williams, and his detractors took pleasure in pointing out a debt (presumably shameful) to a variety of dramatists from Strindberg to Ionesco.

The critical reaction, whatever its verdict, was overexcited and involved Albee in an awkwardly close reaction with the press and public opinion. As both young lion and *enfant terrible*, he was aware of the ambivalence of his position, which, however, he energetically exploited to take a stand as an advocate of a national American theatre, when only months before he had been unknown. Notably he insisted on the responsibility of the critic, and replying to the attacks on *The American Dream* called attention to 'a misuse of the critical function in American press letters'.[2] Was this simply pique, or the irascibility of a young man whose success had been too sudden? The satirical sketch *FAM and YAM* (1960) suggests that Albee had pronounced views on the theatre and his irritation was genuine. The Young American Playwright (YAM) attacks the inertia and complacency of the theatre industry represented by the Famous American Playwright (FAM): 'Here's a list of the villains. The theatre owners . . . the producers . . . the backers . . . the theatre parties . . . the unions . . . the critics . . . the directors . . . and the playwrights themselves . . . That's the list.' The title of the article which YAM is supposedly writing is 'In Search of a Hero'. This was the role in which Albee, no doubt much to his own surprise, had suddenly found himself cast.

Success was not as immediate as it appeared. Albee had written since his youth, composing poetry, attempting fiction, and, despite his disclaimer in the sixties, before *The Zoo Story* he had embarked on a number of experiments in writing for the theatre. If that play arrived at a crux in the history of the American theatre, so too was it a product of a moment of crisis for the author. The sensitive playgoer can tell that certain images and events are too keenly felt and expressed not to be personal. The fact is that there are striking connections between the world of *The Zoo Story* and events in Albee's life. Critics have pounced on this 'confessional' aspect of Albee's writing, frequently finding with scabrous delight images of the writer's homosexuality. In so doing they miss the point of his work and encumber it with sensational implications which the playwright has convincingly disavowed. With hindsight it seems arguable that these reactions were part of a generalised hostility in sections of the press at a time when a less tolerant attitude to individual lifestyles prevailed.

It would, however, be wrong to neglect Albee's biography, for it contains the explanation of some of the plays' emotional resources. The playwright was born on 12 March 1928 in Washington and was abandoned by his natural parents. Two weeks later he was adopted by Reed

Introduction

Albee, a theatrical impressario, and his wife Frances. He was christened Edward Franklin Albee after his adoptive grandfather, founder of the Reed Albee chain of theatres. There is no doubt that the child experienced the tensions of a difficult marriage (Reed Albee's second) and was emotionally handicapped by the knowledge that he was adopted. For his own part he was spoiled and troublesome. Visitors to the Albee home at Larchmount describe how the child was surrounded by servants and had all manner of presents lavished upon him. On Albee's own admission it was a bittersweet childhood.

The ambivalent feelings of the child may have been to some degree the result of the tensions between his parents. Frances Albee was twenty years younger than her husband and determined to lead the luxurious life which the family's wealth allowed. Reed Albee was small and taciturn; his wife tall; imposing, elegant and domineering. Albee's theatre bears the mark of his upbringing. The archetypal American Mommy and Daddy of *The American Dream* and *The Sandbox* betray first-hand experience of the emasculating tensions of the marital couple, and throughout his work the struggle of powerful frustrated women and their indeterminate, morally weak partners is exploited in the creation of his family settings. Another figure from Albee's early years is reflected particularly in these two plays, and in a distinctly more flattering light. His maternal grandmother was, like her adopted grandchild, an outsider to the troubled marriage of the Albees, and across the generations a firm bond was established between the two. In 1959, the year of her death, he was already at work on the plays in which Grandma appears as a character – *The Sandbox*, dedicated to his grandmother, standing as something of a memorial to a relationship which was evidently warm and understanding.

Edward Albee

Albee's own experience as an adopted child is too close to these two plays and also to the Jerry of *The Zoo Story* for it not to be regarded as the impulse behind much of the early writing. Albee's adoption brought him from an early age into daily contact with the world of the theatre; it also created a sensibility that needed to express deep psychological tensions. Written for himself as a thirteenth birthday present, *The Zoo Story* gives vent to his own feelings of abandonment and alienation, as well as working them into a form which gave satisfaction to him as a dramatist. In the later plays this balance altered, but always Albee has considered his writing to be initially a response to a personal need.

There are frequent suggestions of themes which are very like personal obsessions in the dramatist. The foundling child appears in play after play. Gerry in *The Zoo Story*, who tries desperately to make human contact, is abandoned, and has in his room an empty picture frame but no photograph of his lost parents. The adopted child in *The American Dream* is treated as an unsatisfactory piece of merchandise and as a consequence is progressively mutilated to diminish its ability to annoy Mommy and Daddy. In one form or another the loss of the child or parent is behind Albee's plays from the fantasy child of *Who's Afraid of Virginia Woolf?* to the substitute-mother Elizabeth in *The Lady from Dubuque* (1980).

Albee's education was chaotic. He went to a series of schools, like Julia in *A Delicate Balance* (1966), failing to distinguish himself and becoming increasingly difficult. He was finally sent to Valley Forge military academy in the hope that he would benefit from a disciplinarian approach, but again he rebelled. In 1944, despite his record, he was admitted to perhaps the best known of American private schools, Chaote. Here at last his talent and individualism met a warmer response. He had been writing poetry since the age of six and his English teacher encouraged him. He now saw his first work in print. A Texas literary magazine published a poem, and the Chaote School literary magazine published more writing, including *Schism*, a one-act melodrama where the iconoclasm of *The American Dream* can already be felt.

Albee's university education was haphazard. Three terms at Trinity College, Hartford, and briefer registrations at Columbia University and the University of Washington completed his academic career. Although in later life Albee was to reappear in university life as a distinguished lecturer and occasionally as director of his own works, in the early plays there is a clear echo of his dissatisfaction with his professors. There is an edge to the characters of George and Nick in *Who's Afraid of Virginia Woolf?* which might cause a pang to any teacher who had the young Albee in one of his courses. Albee must have been particularly entertained by some of his academic critics who discussed in pedantic detail whether George and Martha were accurate campus figures.

Family tensions, and in particular Frances Albee's opposition to her son's literary ambitions, led to a rupture in 1948, and Albee left home for the more favourable artistic *milieu* of Greenwich Village. He spent a decade in the manner which seems required of the aspiring young American dramatist, taking a variety of jobs in shops, offices and hotels. Most of all he enjoyed his three years as a Western Union telegram messenger, a figure who makes a fleeting appearance in the mind of George in *Who's Afraid of Virginia Woolf?* During this period Albee constantly attended the theatre, seeing particularly the work of Tennessee Williams, and formed close friendships with the novelist Carson McCullers, whose *The Ballad of the Sad Café* he was to adapt in 1963, and William Flanagan, the musician who provided the score for *The Sandbox* and to whom Albee would dedicate *The Zoo Story*.

William Flanagan described how throughout this phase of his life Albee struggled persistently to write. By the age of thirty he had achieved little and was facing a personal crisis. He turned to the theatre, and in a period of three weeks at the beginning of 1958 he wrote *The Zoo Story*. The sense of crisis carries over into the play. The isolation and anguish of the central figure, Gerry, and his strain and alienation from the comfortable world of his antagonist, Peter, reflect the situation of the writer with great immediacy.

The intensity of Albee's view of American society and his passionate attack on complacency and cant did not prove congenial to all his first critics. He indicted a futile materialism in a witty and abrasive style which made the underlying feelings all the more convincing and disconcerting. He seemed to hold up a distorting mirror to society, showing its values to be incoherent and inhuman. With the appearance of *The American Dream* the playwright could be anathematised as nihilist, immoral and defeatist. He was too clearly identifiable with the un-American complications of the new European writing for him not to be assigned immediately to the Theatre of the Absurd. However, the bleakness of Albee's vision was not absurdism nor any species of philosophical nihilism, but the result of a commitment to values he saw neglected or ignored. He was as much an 'angry young man' of American theatre as an absurdist.

His real affinity with the European avant-garde was almost entirely in theatrical method and awareness. It is understandable that Albee should make an appearance in

Martin Esslin's early collection of *Absurd Drama* alongside Arrabal, Adamov and Ionesco. He was not, however, a disciple in any particular school. He naturally absorbed the influence of Beckett, Ionesco and Genet; but equally well he was responsive to the modern classics produced off-Broadway in his formative years: O'Neill, Strindberg and Chekhov, as well as the major works of Williams.

With his metamorphosis from YAM to FAM, Albee as Famous American Playwright lost none of his feeling for the plight of the American stage and in particular his disquiet at the difficulty of staging new work. With his sudden rise to fame, he used his position to point out the villains. His counterblast to his critics was entitled "Which Theater is the Absurd One?" and the message was clear. It was Broadway with its saccharine diet of musicals and occasional anodyne dramas, not the new wave from Europe. The practical response accompanied his campaign in the press, and it was more or less immediate. From 1960 Albee has been heavily involved, professionally, morally and financially in producing new work (including his own) and in sponsoring young writers. Out of his early association with the producers of *The Zoo Story*, Richard Barr and Clinton Wilder, came a steady series of initiatives. The most remarkable of these was the establishment in 1963 of the Playwrights Unit, dedicated to providing full professional productions of new and inexperienced dramatists, in conditions where they could be expected to see their work realised in accordance with their intentions.

Plays submitted (at the rate of about 300 per year) were read by the three directors, and once accepted were given the best feasible production. The playwright could choose the cast and production team he felt his play required, and within the limits of budget and availability it was the job of the unit to provide them, aided by the considerable generosity of colleagues in the profession. The playwright was intimately involved in the planning and production of his work, and at the same time he was protected from the attentions of critics, who were not admitted to the performances. The audience for the unit's productions was drawn from a list, and individuals who failed to attend twice in a season were struck off. There was no payment for admission. As far as possible the playwright was sheltered from the pressures of normal commercial production, and the only criterion of success was artistic.

The Playwrights Unit is cited by Poland and Mailman in *The Off-Off-Broadway Book* alongside Café La Mama, Café Cino and the Open Theatre, among others, as one of the most significant organisations working in the experimental theatre in New York. It was unique in one important respect, reflecting Albee's own convictions: not only did it provide superb facilities for off-off-Broadway performance but it attempted to create an outlet on Broadway itself for the growing stable of playwrights it had reared. The creation of the Playwrights Repertory in 1967 made possible in the following seasons the presentation of an integrated programme of new drama coupled with dance and cinema, using Broadway theatres. In this way, dramatists once sponsored by the Playwrights Unit, such as Sam Shepard, Terrence McNally or LeRoi Jones, were programmed alongside Beckett and Albee himself. Inevitably the financial strain was too great and the venture foundered in 1972, following a further experiment to transport the Repertory to a comfortable suburb outside New York which ended disastrously. Albee's chief contact with new playwrights has since been through his maintenance of his own art centre, where writers and other artists are free to live through a summer and pursue their work.

The scale of Albee's dedication to the theatre is one of the most significant aspects of his life: it is perhaps here that he has found a home and an identity. There can be no doubting his faith in theatre and in its mission in society, and his willingness to make personal sacrifices in pursuit of what is very like an obsession. This needs to be remembered when he is accused of being self-obsessed or preoccupied with a private mythology. The other side to privacy is the degree of risk involved in sharing with a public the images of one's disquiet, and this Albee has not avoided. It is significant that his early ambitions lay in the more 'private' medium of the novel and lyric poetry. He has maintained a steady output of original plays, every two years over the sixties and somewhat more irregularly since then.

Recently, with *Lolita* (1981), Albee has returned to the practice of adaptation which in the sixties seemed to be his chosen way of taking breath between his major plays (*The Ballad of the Sad Café*, 1963; *Malcolm*, 1965; *Everything in the Garden*, 1967). For reasons of space I must neglect these in the following chapters, to provide room for the original works, which are objectively of higher quality. On the margin, as the adaptations seem destined to remain, they are none the less a curious testament to Albee's central position in American theatre as a journeyman – the practitioner of his craft.

Albee has announced that he intends to write on if he is spared until he is seventy; and until his work is complete he discourages his critics from coming to premature conclusions about its significance. What after all, he asks, is 'late' Albee? At the midpoint, however, there is a consistency which is discernible and has to do with the man himself and the way in which his style imprints his sensibility on the plays with increasing concentration.

11

Where his dramatic style will lead he rightly leaves as an open question: it seems certain that he has found his voice and his vocation in the theatre, and the theatre extends for him far beyond the private fantasies of Edward Albee. If there is one prevailing view which does no service to this dramatist, it is the attempt to interpret his work as the theatrical statement of a private message. Albee has statements to make, but they are about the theatre not in it, and it is to these that I shall turn next.

2
Albee on Theatre

Albee has always shared his thoughts on theatre with his public. While he has been vitally concerned with the defence of the theatre and the promotion of its role in society, he has sometimes been too ready to be deflected into a discussion of the 'meaning' of his work. The episode of *Tiny Alice* and its reception in 1964 is illuminating. Calling a press conference is no answer to the problem of obscurity in a dramatist's latest play. If on that occasion Albee seemed to be seeking a dialogue with press and public, it was in part a response to their constant discussion of meaning. Albee has said so much on the subject that his remarks need to be put in perspective.

From the earliest days he has not disguised his interest in the commentaries produced by critics of his plays, and he can in fact be genuinely interested by particular discoveries:

A woman once sent me a paper that she had published on *The Zoo Story*, pointing out, rather beautifully I thought, that Jerry was Christ. And it is true, in *The Zoo Story*, for example, that Peter does deny Jerry three times. He says, I do not understand the point of the dog story three times; and I guess it also true in *Who's Afraid of Virginia Woolf?* Nick says that he does not understand three times – which is another form of denial perhaps. But no deliberate Christian apology.[3]

None of the Christian or other symbolism in his works is intentional, and in discussing this problem Albee has put his finger on the tendency of the critic to latch on to 'symbol' as though it were part of the dramatist's conscious technique, when in fact it is a signpost identified by the critic to show the short cut to a favoured interpretation. Albee astutely senses the distortion that occurs when material of a highly charged kind (the 'symbol' of the critic) is given meanings at anything but a subliminal level:

> it's about time that audiences and critics and just about everybody in general, including playwrights, got rid of this whole notion of the conscious symbolism in realistic or symbolic plays and began to realize that the use of the unconscious in the twentieth century theatre is its most interesting development.[4]

Despite this excellent advice Albee has often been unable to subdue his awareness of the significance of his own work, and thereby has seemed to licence symbolic interpretations and imply the use of techniques of conscious symbolism. His remarks, for example, on *Who's Afraid of Virginia Woolf?* have reinforced an interpretation of the play as political allegory which does not do justice to other meanings which an audience can

14

discover in it. In 1976 he seemed to suggest there was a clear programme to the play:

The play is an examination of whether or not we, as a society, have lived up to the principles of the American Revolution. There's no argument that George and Martha were named after George and Martha Washington.'[5]

Ten years earlier he had been much more tentative in explaining the connection with the Washingtons which had been at the back of his mind and made it clear that this was only one approach to the play, and not the key. His admirers would object that the play is much more than an examination of an issue in the way Albee describes. It has to be said that Albee is not above teasing his public when it comes to the matter of the interpretations of his work. At the same time there is a grain of truth in his mischevious suggestion that he reads the various papers and critical articles on his work and claims as his own those points that he finds to be the most intelligent.

Albee does not, however, incline towards a view of theatre which approves of propaganda or the promotion of any articulated message. It is notable that he confesses to great admiration for Brecht, whom he considers 'a unique artist'; but he asserts that in the case of great plays such as *Mother Courage* or *The Resistible Rise of Arturo Ui* Brecht goes much further than his own theories in creating experiences which involve the audience. *Experience* becomes a key word in Albee's understanding of theatre and its effects. The predominance of a certain viewpoint and intellect is incidental to the sharing of the original private experience of the playwright:

Every play begins as a private personal moment; the success is measured by whether it transcends its original suggestion.[6]

What a writer 'means' by a play is the total experience of the play on an audience, or, to put it more accurately, on the first audience – the audience of himself.[7]

Specific ideas will emerge as part of the spectator's experience, which will not depend upon the perception of a thesis of any kind. The play must not be moulded to fit any conscious point of view.

Albee is none the less a committed writer: his plays challenge the audience and occasionally give a suggestion of thesis through the degree of involvement with the dramatist's social and political experiences. This is, however, not something that the dramatist plans, but an unavoidable condition of his writings: he offers no views but inevitably forces reactions.

I'm not sure that it's the responsibility of a writer to give answers, especially to questions that have no answers – the responsibility of the writer is to be a sort of demonic social critic – to present the world and the people in it as he sees it and say 'Do you like it? If you don't like it change it.' Too many people go to the theatre wanting to be taken out of themselves, to be given an unreal experience. The theatre must always be entertaining, but I think the *Oedipus* is entertaining. I don't think that it's the responsibility of the playwright to present a dilemma and then give its solution, because if he does that, and he is at all concerned with how things are and how people are now, almost inevitably he is going to present a far less puissant dilemma.[8]

Albee's plays become a good deal more interesting if one remembers that it is this 'puissant dilemma' that excites him as a writer, and not an intellectual crux which can be summarily resolved one way or another.

This penchant for dilemma makes Albee a natural man of the theatre. Dilemma is best rendered in producing a coexistence of alternatives. In an art which is founded in action, the crux is where alternative concerns are set in opposition and the choice involves a course of action. In performance, actors and audience share the experience of the alternatives and the resulting tension which is present in all dramatic writing. The degree to which the tensions of the drama can be resolved depends on the particular composition and on its ultimate emotional character. Albee himself experiences problems in the resolution of his works which are intimately concerned with his response as an artist to the anxieties of his age. In his play about art, *Box*, he puts the search for resolution in characteristically musical terms, seeking the movement between 'tension and the tonic'. The musical equivalent of tension is extreme harmonic modulation, easily apparent in discord or dissonance. Resolution involves a return to the tonic, and the home key.

The value of such an experience lies not in the particular ideas which can procure the resolution of dilemma, but in the experience of the tensions themselves. For all its imprecision, and Albee is at pains to point out – even complain about – the imprecision of the theatre, the medium lends itself to the raw stuff of experience. 'I like the sense of immediacy, of the present. I'm not a very good poet, and my prose is tortured. You can get nice tensions going on the stage.'[9] Albee asks his audience to 'suffer the experience'. Ideas arise at the point when the dramatist says 'Do you like it?' An illustration from the rehearsals of

the original production of *Who's Afraid of Virginia Woolf?*
shows Albee alive, practically, to the danger of pat
conclusions getting in the way of the 'gut' experience.
During the final stages he cut out the following speech
George made to Nick:

> Try to learn, teach. I don't hold out much hope for you,
> things being as they are – people. But, and I trust you've
> learnt this by now, the least dishonourable failure is the
> only honourable goal.[10]

Albee has consistently disclaimed a desire to move his
audience on such a conscious level. He sees composition as
largely a natural subconscious process which eases his own
tensions, and is struck by the power of the plays in turn to
make his audiences feel uneasy. The disturbance is basic to
the thinking that may result. The ideas of the play are
embedded in the experience of performance. The failure to
recognise this has misled a good deal of Albee criticism. In
a celebrated piece of vituperation on *Who's Afraid of
Virginia Woolf?* one critic notably fell prey to the false
distinction of effect and meaning. While maintaining that
the play was sustained emotional sensationalism, 'mock
emotions and a mock catharsis', he was able to claim that
the 'message' was

> too clear. In many marriages illusions grow and have to
> be 'exorcised' (this pretentious, crypto-religious word of
> Albee's) in order to save what is left of the partners. But
> the device Albee uses to stage such a truism is once again
> from Ionesco. Patched into a realistic play, it turns the
> whole into a crazy mixture of the obvious and the
> incredible.[11]

Albee's message is nothing of the sort. The critic grasped at the literal and ignored the complexibities of the play, as happens when Albee's critics give way to their spleen. (This same attack contains the famous allegation that the two couples in the play are surrogates for four homosexuals.) For a writer who never writes to accommodate an idea, Albee plainly suffers misunderstanding. It is probably unwise to enter too many interpretative debates with your public, especially when you maintain that the standard of criticism at large is lamentable.

The positive side to Albee's intellectualism is his style, which gives a high priority to the precise values of language. With this comes the love of ideas which can seem like the main emphasis of the plays to those unwilling to 'suffer the experience'. In his radio play *Listening* (1975) Albee gives a hint of the way he understands thought as part of the events in the drama

> THE GIRL: You don't listen . . . Pay attention, rather, is
>   what you don't do. Listen: oh, yes; carefully, to . . .
>   oh, the sound an idea makes . . .
> THE WOMAN: . . . a *thought*.
> THE GIRL: No; an idea.

Ideas are creative happenings. A thought is a report on something past and recorded. (*Quotations from Chairman Mao* exploits this distinction.) Ideas are part of the experience of Albee's work: not thoughts about systems, or philosophies, although these are present; but actual mental activity, cerebration going on onstage and necessarily drawing in the audience. Albee's reported interest in neurology sustains the Girl's explanation of ideas: 'As the chemical thing happens, and then the electric thing, and then the muscle; *that* progression. The response – that

almost reflex thing, the movement, when an idea happens.'
No messages, but ideas and thinking. Albee's view of
theatre is the natural extension of his highly intelligent
sensibility, which in practice is visible in the verbal
acuteness of the encounters in his plays and occasional
questioning of language and self-parody which marks the
writing. This exactness in his control, which has been
accused of mannerism, has been an increasingly evident
aspect of his style in the later works. In Albee's defence it
must be emphasised that language of this sort, like the
peculiar definitions of Harold Pinter's English, comes alive
only when performed as part of a creative process in which
ideas are reworked and rethought by the actors.

This aristocratic use of language has to a degree set
Albee apart, somehow preoccupied by his own elegant but
private meanings, or frankly obscure. He has his own word
for it: 'hermetic'. It is strange to find that this sort of
intellectualism paves the way for a theatre with a political
dimension and implying social comment and criticism; but
Albee has his own concept of political theatre. He rejects
the methods of an earlier generation of dramatists without
rejecting the concept of a political theatre:

> I have never criticized the playwrights of the thirties for
> being dated. I don't like most of them . . . because they
> were aggressively socially conscious and propaganda
> took over from art. . . . Maybe there were easier answers
> in the thirties than there are now in the sixties. . . . We
> were gullible, naïve, and we did not have at that point,
> the potential for destroying ourselves quite so efficiently
> as we do now.[12]

By 1974 Albee could state 'all my plays are political',[13] and
the declaration goes hand in hand with his evident pleasure

in stirring an audience to a reaction. This need not be the result of preaching or propaganda; it is merely inevitable if his individual vision confronts the social and political reality of the time.

The concept of political theatre is one which appears in Albee's separation of his activity in theatre and politics. From time to time he speaks out and he has made no secret of his deep conviction of the need to support the best in liberal democratic values, and to live up to the American revolutionary past. Despite his support for civil liberties, he was nevertheless at pains to divest *The Death of Bessie Smith* of any direct critical and still less propagandist intention, especially when the play was produced in Moscow in 1963. He made it clear that the play related to a precise situation in the USA of 1937, and should not be turned into a criticism of contemporary racial politics.

The Death of Bessie Smith foregrounds private tensions against significant but distanced public events. In a white Southern hospital the central character – the Nurse – entertains any uneasy relationship with an idealistic young doctor – the Intern. She rebuffs his physical advances with a mixture of factitious modesty and contempt for his poverty, which she identifies with his unwillingness to compromise with 'the facts' of the society in which they live. The pressure of that society is felt through the off-stage character of the mayor, who is a patient in the hospital undergoing an undignified minor operation. Albee channels the sexual frustrations of the couple into social and political attitudes. The political is fused with the physical. The chief characters are not individualised by name, but are characterised in their different moral and energetic response to a given political situation. They are impressive and deeply convincing roles, which remain importantly emblematic. One life story is suggested in some detail – that of Bessie Smith herself – and she does not appear.

Albee takes the historical fact of Bessie Smith's death when refused admission to a white hospital after a car accident, and imagines a pattern of tensions in which an outrage of this magnitude can arise. The Nurse sublimates her personal malaise in the expression of tribal hostility to the Orderly, a black whose belief in the progress of civil rights and in the New Deal she derides with an informed cynicism. The Intern's sympathy for the Orderly is similarly mocked through comparisons between the two and their willingness to court favour and financial advantage. While the black orderly works realistically to overcome his disadvantage, the white doctor remains too poor to marry. The role of the Nurse foreshadows the rich contradictions of Martha in *Who's Afraid of Virginia Woolf?* While she baits the Intern for his 'nigger' sympathies, she herself listens to black music, and, when criticised by her father, attacks him for his illusions of status in the second-rate society of the town. The contradictions of the role break out in a howl of protest directed at the Intern and at life in general:

> I am sick of everything in this hot stupid fly-ridden *world*. I am sick of the disparity between things as they are, and as they should be!   . . .   I am tired . . . I am tired of the truth . . . and I am tired of lying about the truth . . . I am tired of my skin . . . I WANT OUT!

These tensions culminate in the fight which is inevitable between the Nurse and the Intern when Bessie Smith is brought to the hospital. The accumulated frustrations of the two roles are released in the threats of the Nurse and the angry response of the Intern, both equally impotent in the face of the fact that Bessie Smith has died long before reaching their hospital. The will and energy of the characters are declared unambiguously in a situation where they can have no personal impact on events. They are denied the opportunity of a symbolic act, and remain the victims of the ancestral attitudes and tensions of their society. Albee's play stresses experience and recognition and ignores easy answers.

His attitude to the production of *Who's Afraid of Virginia Woolf?* in South Africa shows an alternative side of this separation of direct political action and the writing of plays with political implications. The play, he insisted, could only be performed before an integrated audience, after which it was picketed in Port Elizabeth and banned in Johannesburg on the grounds of 'indecency'. Cuts were made, to be followed by demands for further alterations, and finally came the insistence that segregated audiences be restored. As long as the play was open to mixed audiences Albee complied with 'moral' censorship, at whatever the artistic cost. When the political attack became overt, Albee finally withdrew his permission and the tour was cancelled. There was nothing of the comfortable introversion of which he had been accused in his involvement in this fight. This was only confirmed with his letter to the *New York Times* entitled 'Apartheid in the Theatre', in which he indicted his own society for not proving the model it should be: 'for a revolutionary society based upon excellent principles which it would be desirable to export, our performance has been rather poor'.[14]

There is a language for the practice of politics and this Albee has frequently used, as in initiating a boycott of the Athens Festival in protest against the Colonels' coup in 1967, or in his speeches in support of Eugene McCarthy's presidential campaign in 1968. But theatre does not have to adopt that language to be political. If Albee has a political effect it must be present in the way the audience views itself and the world.

> When I write a play I am interested in changing the way people look at themselves and at their lives. I have never written a play which was not essentially political. But it is useless to attack details or the conscious level. What you must lay siege to is the unconscious.[15]

The idea of political theatre operating at an unconscious level does not commend Albee to a range of critics who do not find his politics hard-edged enough, and think that the impression emerging from his plays is naïve or sentimental. This is the view taken by Richard Schechner (the influential editor of the *Drama Review*) and others, to whom Albee has replied by repeating his assertion that the audience must be approached through the unconscious, as much as through statements on the conscious level. Charles Marowitz has similarly found Albee's political position 'assumed and unconvincing' in *Who's Afraid of Virginia Woolf?* and has concluded that *The American Dream*, 'overtly social and satiric, reveals more about the author's private mythology than it does about the society he is ostensibly attacking'.[16] Marowitz felt that the central character of the *American Dream* – the All-American boy – was 'a marvellous opportunity for satire' which Albee did not develop. The point here is surely that Albee *does* have his private mythologies, but his method involves sharing these with his audience, at which point they can have an impact within its political experience. He never intends the political dimension of his work to be abstract and independent of his personal sensibilities. If the boy in *The American Dream* is left as a shell, it is because Albee is dramatising a soulless aspect of American society; he does not wish to involve himself in its sociology.

Albee's concept of political drama is more readily explained by his ideas on the general effect of the medium, and the type of theatre he practises. His conviction that the unconscious is the target of the dramatist is consistent with a feeling for the theatre as a private and above all an intimate experience. There is more than an echo of Strindberg and the Intimate Theatre movement of the early years of the present century in the way Albee's ideal is expressed:

> I have to say that I am absolutely opposed to that conception of the theatre defined as a great collective experience lived in common with the public, by a thousand spectators who react on each other by the warmth of their bodies, and inept comments like that. The ideal production of a play would be to have all the actors in a room with an INVISIBLE spectator whom the actors would not be able to see.[17]

While this is overstated, it expresses in other terms Albee's dislike of what he calls 'flashy' theatre. Thus the spectaculars of Broadway are anathema to him, as well as the spuriously brilliant imports, among which he numbers *Rosencrantz and Guildenstern are Dead* and *Marat–Sade*. He puts emphasis on a fine perception of performance which is more likely with a theatre whose means are restrained. In such a theatre he emphasises the role of aural and musical values, placing particular reliance on the word. *Box* and *Quotations from Chairman Mao*, for example, he thought might make a better effect if read first, and at one stage he certainly believed that *Tiny Alice* was clearer to a reader than a spectator. This should be construed not as a manifesto for armchair theatre, but rather as a pointer to certain values in his own compositions which depend on the word as a physical experience, like the tone in music:

> a play, though it does exist physically on the stage, and can be read is enormously aural. And the structure of a play is apprehended in the mind by the ear, very much the way that a musical composition is.'[18]

Small wonder that Albee prefers a scale and style of performance where the audience can attend to the detail of language, undistracted by the auditorium. His concept is well formulated by Strindberg, a dramatist to whom Albee has been often likened, in his definition of chamber theatre: 'The conception of chamber music transferred to drama. The intimate action, the highly significant motif, the sophisticated treatment.'[19] Those three terms are highly relevant to the style of work Albee has developed. The theatre he imagines, and demonstrably the works he has produced, demand such an intimate theatre both in terms of performance and audience attention.

In general Albee has advocated an art theatre as opposed to 'rough' and 'popular' theatres and certainly to the escapist entertainment of most Broadway productions. He has unhesitatingly condemned the theatrical life of Broadway, arguing that producers are largely engaged in the import trade, when they are not reviving forgotten musicals. The problems are not all in New York, he argues, for America as a whole has no theatre culture. But, in the face of a tradition which, he argues, goes back no further than Tennessee Williams and the later plays of O'Neill, the need is all the greater to foster the serious American theatre, which is to be found as yet fighting for survival off- and off-off-Broadway.

The involvement in the Broadway debate has a twofold importance for Albee. On the one hand he is a 'Broadway' writer himself, in that he has repeatedly submitted his work to the vicissitudes of production and criticism there; on the other he sees a matter of principle. New York remains the capital of American theatre, and, despite the proliferation of repertory and campus theatres, New York has a responsibility when it comes to quality and innovation, as Albee emphasises, usually in order to point out how New York fails the nation and Broadway fails New York. But his feelings go further. These are not the views merely of a professional anxious to defend his trade and see a free and fair marketplace for his products. Albee has a philosophy of the theatre which entrusts it with vital functions in society. His concern for theatre derives from his concern for society.

Theatre is always in one important sense contemporary: it cannot live without the recognition of its society, and without this it easily dies. Being the most contemporary of the arts, it is the intimate reflection of its time, for the people of its time. Albee's view of the theatre derives its coherence from his understanding of this relationship: 'The function of the theatre as a form of art is to tell us who we are: that is its first value; and the health of the theatre depends on the degree of self-knowledge we wish to have.'[20]

The theatre as *art* – not as political tract – has the vital function he describes. It is the source of a dialogue between a creative and a receptive sensibility. Albee's art theatre can in this way be equated with the political theatre he claims to write, where the place accorded to the theatre as art indicates the mentality of the society that is its audience. Such a political theatre is both an invitation to change, and the proof of the openness of the society to itself. George's cryptic lines in *Who's Afraid of Virginia Woolf?* sound unmistakably like the author's view: 'you make government and art, and realize that they are, must be, both the same'.

Thus, for Albee, theatre is both personal and political, public and private, art and commitment. He infuses his plays with his private experience to such a degree that hostile criticism becomes personal attack. Given the difficulty of his relationship with both press and public in New York, one might expect that he would occasionally seek other theatres in which to present new work. There can be little doubt that any of the major repertory theatres would be able and willing to mount an Albee premiere. Why therefore does he stick to Broadway and risk the sort of failure which overtook *The Lady from Dubuque*? The answer seems to lie in Albee's insistence on the value of dramatic art and the role of the national theatre. It would be too easy for Albee to retreat off-Broadway, but he chooses to fight his battle for serious theatre in the place where victory counts for most. On Broadway.

3
Albee in the Theatre: 'Tiny Alice'; 'Box' and 'Quotations from Chairman Mao'; Intimate Theatre

Albee's career as a writer has been accompanied by an increasing concern with the practical medium of theatre. From the outset he championed theatre in America, and has actively promoted new work, both his own and that of other, predominantly younger, dramatists. In more recent years he has become active as the director of his own plays. This is consistent with a shift in the position he adopts towards performance. In 1963 he felt that the ideal performance was the one he had experienced in his own imagination: 'There is only one true, correct, hard, ideal performance of a play, and that is mine, and I saw it when I was writing.'[21] By 1978, when he was engaged in a tour of five of his early plays, he was no longer prepared to leave the 'ideal performance' as the property of the writer, and evidently felt dissatisfied with the sort of direction to be seen in the theatre: 'I think I can get clarity and precision by directing myself. The direction may not be flashy but I'm not really interested in flash.'[22] The qualities which Albee speaks of complement his articulate style of writing.

Although to many his plays are so literate they seem to offer as much to the reader as to the theatregoer, one should not confuse theatricality with what Albee calls 'flash'. His preferences are made clear in his reaction to the famous Peter Book production of Peter Weiss's *Marat–Sade*, which he considered 'a rotten play . . . with a big, showy, splashy production'.[23]

Albee's scripts are highly verbal, but they are also careful blueprints for a theatrical performance, with detailed indications of how he wishes the play to emerge in performance. This is apparent in his use of stage directions, which allow his theatrical vision to emerge. And 'vision' is what he supplies. The degree of precision he insists on varies, but his indications describe the essential theatrical requirements. So for *The Death of Bessie Smith* he describes a possible scene: 'The set for this play will vary, naturally, as stages vary – from theatre to theatre. So, the suggestions put down below, while they may serve as a useful guide, are but a general idea – what the author "sees".' Often Albee indicates his setting in similar terms – as a visualised performance area:

> I see a fairly short wall, and two side walls angling from it to the proscenium . . . (*Counting the Ways*)

> I see the environment as uncluttered, perhaps with a Bauhaus feel. No decorator has been at work; what we see is the taste of the occupants. I think the predominant colour should be light gray. . . .
>
> (*The Lady from Dubuque*)

Often his requirements are so lacking in 'flash' that he contents himself with a brief statement of the environment:

The scene is the living-room of a house on the campus of
a small New England College.

> (*Who's Afraid of Virginia Woolf?*)

THE SCENE. The living-room of a large and well-
appointed suburban house. Now.   (*A Delicate Balance*)

Despite the brevity of these indications there is a visual
imagination at work, as can be seen in the handling of key
moments in the action of the plays. An example of Albee
visualising the scene is the entrance of Nick and Honey in
Act I of *Who's Afraid of Virginia Woolf?*:

> GEORGE (*moving towards the door*): All right, love . . .
> whatever love wants. Isn't it nice the way some people
> have manners, though, even in this day and age? Isn't
> it nice that some people won't just come breaking into
> other people's houses even if they do hear some
> sub-human monster yowling at 'em from inside . . .?
> MARTHA: SCREW YOU!
> *Simultaneously with Martha's last remark,* GEORGE *flings
> open the front door.* HONEY *and* NICK *are framed in the
> entrance.*

In *Who's Afraid of Virginia Woolf?* and *A Delicate Balance*
Albee does not specify the stage setting, nor the
relationships of elements in the set, whose functions are
made clear as the action progresses. In each case Albee
asks the director and designer to create a particular sort of
environment, and to this extent his imagination is working
both socially and theatrically. For *Who's Afraid of Virginia
Woolf?* Albee and Alan Schneider, his director,
transcended the natural interior in an attempt to create a
disturbing sense of a cave or refuge. His instructions are

more explicit in *The Sandbox*, *The American Dream*, and still more clear in *Tiny Alice* and *Box* and *Quotations from Chairman Mao*. *The Sandbox* requires a precise positioning of chairs, a music stand and the sandbox with a child's pail and shovel. The scenic requirements are laid out with great clarity. *The American Dream* demands no more than a sketch of a living-room – a commonplace to match the clichés in which the play deals. In the later two plays Albee makes a more conspicuous effort to develop his use of the plastic quality of the stage medium.

Tiny Alice: Enigmatic Images

In *Tiny Alice* Albee is keenly aware of the colour and texture of images, as in the opening scene, where the Cardinal receives his guest the lawyer in his garden. Colours, red and black, are determined by the characters' costumes and echoed in the jokes on the caged birds at their side: 'cardinals . . .?' The play produces images of a similar quality in the unmasking of the 'aged' Miss Alice, and the final *pietà* after the death of Julian. This experimentation goes beyond the use of the stage as a decorative medium. Meanings are created through the combination of the audience's sensual experiences and intellectual and emotional responses. One possible ending for *Tiny Alice* demonstrates the way a particular meaning and experience would be created for an audience:

Originally when I was thinking about the play, before I got to writing it down, I was going to have him [Julian] tied to a large table, a leg of which would break, and then he would be, as the leg broke and the table angled out onto the floor, in a cruciform position. . . . the last scene of the play should seem as though he is in the attic closet, enclosed, as a child in the dark, and that no one would come. There are a number of things you can't do on the stage. I suppose, ideally, Julian would have been thrust right into the lap of the audience for the last scene. After the fact, I even considered, or rather thought about, how nice it would have been if I could have had some of the play on film in order to bring Julian much closer.[24]

Albee is concerned with the problem of how he can focus attention to produce the effect of close-up. A student of his plays can supply an answer to the problem from an examination of the playwright's own solution elsewhere. Albee's real close-ups are in the quasi-soliloquies he gives to his characters at the moment of crisis. In the theatre most often the relationship of stage to audience is fixed, and the performer moves within these limits. However, human vision and attention is highly selective, and, as the audience focuses on the soliloquy more and more closely, there is a distinct illusion of being drawn into the performance. This is something that Albee instinctively achieved from his earliest writing. In *Tiny Alice* he develops the plastic medium of the stage so far that he overloads his composition with significant visual material.

Given the hostility of the reaction to *Tiny Alice* the author deserves some sympathetic understanding of his experiments. By developing the image he aims at a greater potential effect, than, say, in *Who's Afraid of Virginia Woolf?*, where some of the poignancy of the experience may have been blunted by the familiar style. This would explain Charles Marowitz's criticism: '*Who's Afraid of Virginia Woolf?* is a generalized social indictment, and it is this very generality that so weakens its case. Its psychological tensions are real enough; its political attitude, assumed and unconvincing.' Marowitz is unsympathetic to politics which are personal and felt, rather than explicit or didactic. Albee earns this harsh treatment because the surface naturalism is so rich as to diffuse the effect and impact of the action. Marowitz reacts to the emotional battle but misunderstands the grounds on which it is fought: 'First-class up-dated Strindberg perhaps, but very bogus Ibsen.'[25] Ibsen is a dramatist whom Albee does not admire greatly and to whom he claims he finds it difficult to respond.

In *Tiny Alice* Albee attempts to gain greater control over the language of the stage by working in a more deliberately abstract and symbolic way. However, as he developed a new style he was addressing himself to his old public, who identified Albee with the post-Strindbergian sex drama that had thrilled them, apparently to the exclusion of the dramatist's deeper meanings. The reaction to *Tiny Alice* was such that Albee felt impelled to call a press conference to examine the confusion his play had caused. The note he has left in the printed text recalls these initial difficulties, and confirms his doubtful success. While maintaining the work to be 'quite clear', he suggests that the clarity is demonstrable on reading rather than attending the play. The intellectual points which *Tiny Alice* was making were apparent to the playwright, and he felt that the open-minded reader would see what was intended. Albee discussed in much less detail the theatrical quality of his work. In the end he asks of his audience one thing: 'to suffer the experience'. In *Tiny Alice* the truth about his writing is clear: his plays are not statements. They are theatrical experiences to be undergone.

Different theatrical experiences have different degrees of intellectual exactness or clarity: *Tiny Alice* is a rich and exciting piece of theatre but with no simple points to make.

It demonstrates the power of the author's theatrical imagination and is in part about imagination and its role in human life. It is also a translation of Albee's private images into a full theatrical expression, where previously he had relied extensively on language and particularly on narration to communicate these to his audience.

The play, recalling, as it does to the scholar, Julian the Apostate, has to do with acts of faith, and this key notion may be borne in mind in examining its life in the theatre – a medium whose illusions are dependent on the creation of particular states of 'faith' in the audience. The play is conceived a little in the manner of a thriller with an elaborate arrangement of deceit and pretence. Albee both plays games with his audience (in the best sense – he joins in the play) and plays upon the unprepared reactions he can produce from the arrangement of images he devises for the stage. The theme of faith has a real viability when expressed through such an ambitious design of pretence and imagination. The taste can be judged from the first two scenes.

I.i concerns the meeting of two characters, neither being given a name. They are Cardinal and Lawyer, apparently representative of God and Mammon. In I.ii another character is introduced and his name is a joke: he is called and is Butler. The only character who is named and individualised in the play is Julian, creating the impression that the other roles are a theatrical projection of his inner turmoil. Although the play does not function entirely according to an expressionist idea of the stage events as viewed through the subjective experience of the central character, Albee derives something from this tradition of writing in the theatre. It is in all probability his most important debt to Strindberg, but it is only one possibility in a complex use of the stage images. They are not the figures in Julian's childish nightmares, important though these are to the themes of the play. The characters are written in a style to give a superficial naturalism which commands the audience's belief. On top of this Albee's writing is repeatedly applied to questioning the image. The Lawyer and the Cardinal are stage ikons – easily read and grasped by the spectator, but the roles develop grotesquely in contrast with the two functions of Church and Law represented. There is here a reminder of Genet's liking for theatricality of these functions and their ritual possibilities in developing a ceremonial theatre. In a different way Albee exploits the figures, and undermines them. It is the Lawyer who reminds Julian, 'I have learned . . . never to confuse the representatives of a . . . thing with the thing itself.'

This remark has its relevance for the audience's understanding of the action but it also indicates how Albee is developing the theatrical experience of the spectator and attempting to integrate the two. He obliges the audience to experience events and then radically revalue the experience. This is a fundamental characteristic of the medium of theatre, but is not always developed to a point where the audience is obliged to recognise the artificiality of the medium itself. It is of course a marked characteristic of the theatre of the seventeenth century, and if *Tiny Alice* earns any qualification it might be as a Jacobean work.

There is a baroque taste at work in some of the shifts of image which assail the audience, as in the moment, reminiscent of Bergman's *Hour of the Wolf*, where Miss Alice, first described as a young woman, then appearing as a 'withered crone', subsequently puts aside her stick and peels off her 'face'. The image *is* strange and possibly obscure, explicable as an aspect of isolation and fear in the central character, rather than an attempt to make a rational point. The striking image in which Julian 'finds' himself in Alice before his marriage is another such case. The actress must wear a costume with deep sleeves so that, while Julian kneels before her, she, with her back to the audience, can enfold him 'in her great wings'. The image has an affective power one could compare to a similar moment at the conclusion of Ibsen's *Peer Gynt*, and likewise has a religious overtone despite the added sensuality of the moment. The same sort of imagination is at work in the concluding image of Calvary. The instruction is given: 'Goes to him; they create something of a *pietà*.' The final moment reasserts Albee's theme of the crucifixion.

His arms are wide, should resemble a crucifixion.
'. . . JULIAN *dies, head bows, body relaxes some, arms stay wide in the crucifixion. Sounds continue thusly: thrice after the death . . . thump* thump *thump* thump *thump* thump. *Absolute silence for two beats. The lights on* JULIAN *fade slowly to black. Only then, when all is black, does the curtain slowly fall.*

This image concludes a scene of abandonment and recalls the account given earlier of Julian's experience as an injured child, waiting alone in the dark for his grandfather to come to his help. The Calvary is preceded by Gethesamene, and the similarity of Christ's agony in the garden to Julian's confrontation with reality is unmistakable. While the Lawyer and Alice analyse the passion in abstract terms, Julian appears unwilling to remain and face the isolation to come. The Lawyer calmly shoots him, while Alice protests he would have remained to face the outcome all the same. Albee presents the ultimate confrontation with reality in the evocation of death – and in its most recognisable image of all, Calvary.

His overwhelming interest in visual effect is confirmed by the use of an on-stage model of the castle in which the action is deemed to take place. As the final crisis approaches, a light moves through the rooms of the castle approaching the corresponding room to the one in which Julian is suffering his last agony. The action going on 'in another dimension' has its effect within the narrative, but its real impact is felt as a visible reflection of the stage and its events. It creates the feeling of the box-within-box of the Chinese puzzle, and draws attention to the artifice of the stage. Scenic elements are explored for the way in which they can stimulate and provoke the audience, not merely for the simple efficiency with which they provide an environment for the dramatic narrative. Albee's on-stage model with its 'mouse' inside, expressing Alice, truth, reality, whatever it is, is perhaps not a very happy invention in terms of the interpretation of the play. It looks as though it is expected to carry an intolerable burden of meaning. It is just as important, however, in exposing the pretence of the stage by playing with the value of images. While the deceptions to which Julian is subjected at the hands of Butler, the Lawyer and Alice supply one justification of the theatricality of Albee's staging, on a completely different level he is playing with the impact of the visual. The effect of the last scene can be compared with that of the first, where the idea of the set within a set is suggested in a witty fashion by having caged birds observed from the stage by the Cardinal and the crow-like Lawyer.

This play and its problems will be better judged when there is a fuller history of production. Christopher Bigsby expressed the general view when he wrote that Albee 'has presumably accepted the challenge of communicating directly to an audience, and in this he has patently failed'.[26] Albee's own assertion that the play is clear on the page seems to confirm the idea that he intends direct communication and has not experimented in some of the more indirect ways which the theatre medium affords. His comment really expresses the dilemma which results from wedding a prolific theatrical imagination to an overarticulate investigation of complex metaphysics. Albee's characters, for all their passion, are sometimes too articulate to take their places easily within the theatrical images he constructs. We therefore have a straining for expression in both theatrical and discursive terms, and too much meaning makes for confusion.

Box and *Quotations from Chairman Mao*: Effective Images

The strain is never felt in the experimental *Box* and *Quotations from Chairman Mao*, two linked plays written in 1968. There is an interesting similarity with one of the chief images of *Tiny Alice*. Albee explained that he had once been struck by a newspaper report of a man who had been imprisoned in a room within yet another room – a sort of Chinese-box puzzle. Thus the box-within-a-box effect of *Tiny Alice* returns in a suitably Chinese form.

The set for the first play, *Box*, is as follows:

> the outline of a large cube. The side facing the audience is open, but we should see the other five sides clearly, therefore the interior of the cube should be distorted . . . but the angles of distortion should not be so great as to call attention to themselves and destroy the feeling of a cube.

The only character, Voice, who is heard over the theatre's sound system, meditates upon the box and upon its fashioning: 'Many arts: all craft now . . . and going further. But *this* is solid, perfect joins . . . good work.' In the meditation on the set, the linked ideas of the box and art – another way of making things – are contrasted with the decline of the West: 'If only they had *told* us! When it was clear that we were not only corrupt – for there is nothing that is not, or little – but corrupt to the selfishness, to the corruption, that we should die to keep it . . . go under rather than. . . .' The box set is on the one hand an abstract which expresses the general idea of form and craft, and on the other serves as a space with human significance, just as the theatre space does. Voice considers its potential, using turns of phrase suggestive of past civilised values: 'room for a *sedia d'ondalo* . . . *And* room enough to walk around in, take a turn.'

When the set changes for *Quotations from Chairman Mao*, the deck of an ocean liner appears within the box frame of the earlier play. However, in contrast with *Tiny Alice*, here the theatrical metaphor requires no explanation. Once again Albee maintains that his methods are simple, but on this occasion his claim is better supported by the purity of his theatrical approach: 'they *are* simple once they are experienced relaxed and without a weighing of their methods against more familiar ones'.

Box works rather like a musical fantasia. The audience enjoys the most simplified of spectacles: the contemplation of the set as an art object in theatrical space, while Voice extemporises on the relationship of such an experience to the reality outside: 'when art begins to hurt, it's time to look around. Yes it is.'

Albee has explained that *Quotations* derived from *Box*, and the text bears this out. The abstract encounter in *Box* is developed in more realistic terms in the play-within-a-play, inasmuch as the ideas which preoccupy Voice are expanded and developed through a cast of Chairman Mao, the Minister, the Old Woman, and the Long-Winded Lady, each of whom allows the dramatist to particularise and characterise ideas. The realism is only relative. Albee uses his characters for highly specific effects, and they depend on his sense of the theatre image. They are not presented in relationships observed from life. The assembly has an instantaneous theatrical impact: the empty box is filled with the deck of the liner and on it the characters are distributed in controlled characteristic attitudes. The familiar oriental figure, masked or made up to resemble Mao as closely as possible, stands looking out at the audience amid his incongruous Western companions. The Old Woman is differentiated by being set apart 'in one place, upon something'. She is shabby, with a bag containing fruit and canned food, and a spoon, fork and can-opener, so that she may eat through the performance. She speaks directly to the audience alone, but she must react 'in agreement' with Mao from time to time. The other two characters are more appropriately seated in deck chairs; the Minister must pay sympathetic attention to the Long-Winded Lady. He has no lines, while she is directed to speak for herself, occasionally to the Minister, but never in direct address to the audience.

The visual impression made by the characters is intended to be quite immediate. Costume and make-up are required to typify a certain social role. The Minister keeps busy with 'pipe and pouch and matches'. The actor should be 'seventy or so' and have 'white or gray hair, a clerical collar. A florid face would be nice. If a thin actor is playing the role, however, then make the face sort of gray-yellow-white.' The Long-Winded Lady must produce above all a particular effect of class. Visual details are subordinate to this. Albee says, 'I care very little about how she looks so long as she looks very average and upper middle-class. Nothing exotic, nothing strange.' One cannot help feeling as Albee assembles this unlikely cast within the box set that he is intending a theatrical pun. The familiar formula of a quartet of players in a standardised box setting is taken and turned to an unconventional purpose.

Perhaps most curious is the way in which Albee organises the performance within the visual frame of the box. He intends to balance the performances in certain ways, and to this end he makes conscious use of the direction and type of speech he gives to each character. Any suggestion of a naturalistic interaction is minimal and the play develops primarily as the extrapolation of the stage image. The play has a dramatic action in that the different characters make statements in different styles about their different attitudes to the world. The degree to which these positively interact is limited. The effectiveness is in the interaction within the audience's mind, where the fragments of Albee's composition make their meanings.

The word 'composition' finally expresses the key aspects of Albee's stagecraft. He is highly conscious of visual composition, and here he isolates the visual possibility and presents a careful arrangement of characters. The second compositional aspect derives from the first in that the restrictions on stage movement and interaction, and the limitations on action, emphasise the musical nature of the composition.

It is not until *Counting the Ways* that Albee returns to such a theatrical presentation of his images. In the later play the tone is quite different. It is a vaudeville, but its visual effect depends upon the arrangement of a few props within an abstract black box set, and the composition of a series of solos and duos for the two players. Behind the humour of vaudeville presentation – a series of acts each introduced by a sign descending from the flies – there is a theatrical strength and confidence in the shaping of the stage images and in the composition of the two performances as 'acts' in the old music-hall or vaudeville sense.

The progression from *Tiny Alice* to *Box* and *Quotations from Chairman Mao* to *Counting the Ways* shows how important the control of the stage medium is to Albee's method. To some these plays are the demonstration of his eclectic approach to the theatre, but they are in fact the extension of his fundamental awareness into particular compositional experiments. However abstract *Box* may seem in comparison with the full-blown passion of *Who's Afraid of Virginia Woolf?*, it is just as deeply felt. Thematically it has much in common with the earlier work, and both plays employ similar meditations on the decline of Western civilisation. Voice's affirmations of the role of art carries the same idea of loss as the speeches of George to Nick. What differs is the obvious art dimension in which *Box* is written: 'And if you go back to a partita . . . ahhhhh, what when it makes you cry? Not from the beauty of it, but solely that you cry from loss . . . so precious.' *Box* is in its very conception a theatrical manifesto, actively recording Albee's concern with and for the medium of theatre.

Intimate Theatre

I have concentrated to this point on the way in which Albee has developed his awareness of the plastic medium of the stage. It seems at the same time that his feeling for the actor is diminishing as he places the performance within stricter limits. To a degree this is true. He never again writes roles like those of Martha and George, where sheer flamboyance

43

and naked personality are required, and permitted. Just as he has become progressively more interested in direction, he has increasingly asserted authorial control in his writing since *Who's Afraid of Virginia Woolf?* With the production of *Tiny Alice* Albee made demands for a certain type of performer able to deal with the language he was writing, and he was led to require among other English classically trained actors and actresses. *Tiny Alice* was performed by John Gielgud and Irene Worth in the two main roles, and the cast included William Hutt, who has had a distinguished career as a Shakespearian actor with the Festival Theatre at Stratford, Ontario. While there is no doubt that Albee's writing depends increasingly on the performer's control and technique, it is no less intense. He has always exploited the vulnerability of performers on a stage, and his sensitivity to this aspect of the theatre is what makes his writing peculiarly effective. The recurring ideas of abandonment and loss in plays are directly expressed by the dramatic and theatrical stresses on his performers. One sees in the adaptation of *Malcolm*, from the novel by James Purdy, the attraction that the same theme had for Albee in the work of another man, and why he was convinced that the book could adapt successfully to theatrical presentation. Purdy's story draws Malcolm through a series of encounters in which his innocence and abandonment are exploited by the representatives of a corrupt society. It is a short step to conceive Malcolm as a role for an actor whose very medium is his vulnerability, required as he is to act before the gaze of an audience of strangers.

In the earliest plays Albee was fortunate in writing for the emerging off-Broadway theatre, where the scale of resources puts great emphasis on the performers. He is at his best handling duos in the earliest plays. The prime example is *The Zoo Story*, but in *The Sandbox* or *The*

Death of Bessie Smith, in *The American Dream* or in *Who's Afraid of Virginia Woolf?*, he writes extensive duologue. This is unremarkable except that it reflects an off-Broadway characteristic made a virtue. In small theatres and still more in café theatres and other marginal situations, small casts encounter the audience in a particularly close relationship. *The Zoo Story* exemplifies the potential of this small-scale intimate theatre.

The set is minimal: a pair of park benches. There is no distinct requirement for any further elements in the staging, and in many ways the play invites an open or arena staging. However it is set, the play is well adapted to the minuscule stages Albee knew when he was writing. The audience is extremely close and cannot be ignored; light spills, and the watching faces cannot be lost in an anonymous darkness. Even the noise of the audience and its movement is audible to the performer. At this sort of distance the audience is extremely sensitive to the tensions of the play, and to the tension which accompanies performance. For all concerned, the excitement of the theatre is manifest in the frankness of the encounter between the play and its public.

In *The Zoo Story* the theatrical situation adds impact to the confrontational method of the dramatist. The comfortable public persona of Peter is faced with the unpredictable and consequently threatening outsider Jerry. From the outset the play develops a recognisable social tension resulting from the trampling of social convention and the invasion of privacy. Peter occupies a park bench and wishes to read; Jerry insists on conversation, and gradually forces Peter to reveal details of his private life. Albee caricatures Peter's family so that the aggression in the role of Jerry can easily be transmuted into satire.

JERRY: Where do you live? (PETER *is reluctant*.) Oh, look; I'm not going to rob you, and I'm not going to kidnap your parakeets, your cats, or your daughters.

The raw violence of Jerry's intrusion feeds the audience's reflex judgement of his behaviour as a threat, and the play naturally gathers in tension as he challenges Peter's right to the bench he occupies. While this contest is the ostensible issue up to the closing moments of the play, Peter is also obliged to listen to Jerry's story about his visit to the zoo. On one level this is an extension of the original intrusion, but it also has a hypnotic effect on Peter. The story has a content he does not wish to hear. It is a story of abandonment and loss, and in itself is an appeal to the society that Peter personifies.

Jerry explains the loss of his parents and describes the complete alienation of the 'permanent transient' that he has become. Where the detail of Peter's life is deliberately mocked, Jerry enters into confidences which both express the abandonment he feels and overstep the bounds of restraint society imposes on its members.

I've never been able to have sex with, or, how is it put? . . . make love to anybody more than once. Once; that's it . . . Oh, wait; for a week and a half, when I was fifteen . . . and I hang my head in shame that puberty was late . . . I was a h-o-m-o-s-e-x-u-a-l.

The strength of the play lies in the way in which Albee maintains the aggressive stance of Jerry while leading his audience to an experience of what his violence signifies. The burden of the story of the dog is that a relationship built on mistrust and violence is at least a relationship and preferable to indifference – the end result in the story when

46

Jerry meets violence with violence and attempts to kill his adversary. Thus the concluding image of the play, with its strong impression of Calvary, is at one and the same time both a violent demand and the ultimate in self-sacrifice. Jerry demands that Peter fight for his exclusive society and forces him to take a knife he has produced, much to Peter's horror. Jerry then impales himself as Peter holds out the blade to ward off attack. The implications of the play are deeply disturbing, and arise out of the careful presentation of physical violence within the most intimate concept of theatre. Ultimately Albee requires that his audience experience at close hand the contradiction of a society in which contact can be established only through the most animal expression: violence. Jerry looks for love and fails to find it; the least he achieves, however, is to raise Peter from the level of a vegetable and suggest the beginnings of a community. 'It's all right,' he says, 'you're an animal. You're an animal, too.'

Albee's concentration on essentials is most clear in his little play *The Sandbox*, where again with a minimal staging he dramatises his personal loss. The effect is peculiarly intimate, given the use made of the theatre, and the explicit subject: the death of his grandmother. The work is striking for the freedom with which Albee mixes styles and means, combining the burlesque formalism of his absurdist Mommy and Daddy with the graceful naturalism of Grandma, all three characters being clearly drawn from *The American Dream*, which he was writing at the time his grandmother died. In addition Albee creates a positive suggestion of music theatre, with the use of an on-stage musician who responds as a character to suggestions from Grandma. The cast is completed by the Young Man, who clumsily explains to Grandma that he is an actor – as yet without a name. Throughout the play he performs exercises – movements which foreshadow his role as the Angel of Death in the concluding moments of the play.

The arrangement of the stage suggests a performance space rather than any scene, and underlines the concept of the play as the passing rites performed as a conscious game. The vacuous Mommy and Daddy occupy two chairs facing the audience, while a third faces in from stage left towards a music stand for the Musician. Up-stage centre against a simple lit background is the child's sandbox, to which Mommy and Daddy carry Grandma at the outset. Here she plays out the dementing role in which Mommy casts her until she takes her cue to shovel sand over herself and 'plays dead.(!) [*sic*]'.

The artificiality of performance is highlighted as part of a burlesque process which manifests the insincerity of Mommy's attitudes and the absence of any initiative at all in the role of Daddy. Mommy's grief at Grandma's passing is indicated clearly as stage emotion. When a sound-effect is heard, Mommy reminds Daddy tearfully, 'It was an off-stage rumble . . . and you know what that means . . . It means the time has come for poor Grandma. . . .' In a different fashion altogether Grandma and the Young Man consider performance as an act performed with care and compassion, albeit with doubtful competence, to comfort her when she finds that the game she played mischievously for Mommy has overtaken her and she can no longer move. Grandma tells the Young Man of the life in which she struggled through an early widowhood only to be taken 'off the *farm* and moved to a big town house' and, like a domestic animal, given a blanket, a dish and a place under the stove. The speech confirms the loss of love in the family, which is so visible in the desiccated style Albee adopts for the roles of Mommy and Daddy. His own fondness for Grandma is quite evident in the depth of affection the role projects, and in the apologetic way in which the Young Man, almost as the spokesman for the theatre and its performance, struggles to play out, as best he can, this very real tribute to Albee's own grandmother.

> THE YOUNG MAN: I am the Angel of Death. I am . . . uh . . . I am come for you.
> GRANDMA: What . . . wha . . . (*then, with resignation*) . . . ohhhh . . . ohhhh, I see.
> THE YOUNG MAN *bends over, kisses* GRANDMA *gently on the forehead*
> GRANDMA (*her eyes closed, her hands folded on her breast again, the shovel between her hands, a sweet smile on her face*): Well, that was very nice, dear.

It is curious that in comparing Albee to Strindberg critics have not commented on their similar preference for this sort of intimate theatre. Consciously or not, Albee has created his own chamber theatre, writing concentrated exchanges between players to be watched with very close attention. Strindberg speaks of 'the concept of chamber music transferred to drama. The intimate action, the highly significant motif, the sophisticated treatment.' These ideas square well with Albee's practice, and with his concern with the compositional process. In many ways Albee creates the quality of chamber music: *Seascape* is very much a quartet piece; Tobias's long speech at the conclusion of *A Delicate Balance* is described as an 'aria', expressing the way the performer detaches himself from the limitations of the stage naturalism. One suspects that Albee has in mind a musical performance when he describes his writing as composition. The musician is placed in a situation in which his personality is on display with no support from the elements of theatre. His 'characterisation' grows from the interpretative and technical aspects of his performance. This is equally the case in much of Albee's writing, where the use of the stage is extremely restrained and understated, while the actor is pushed forward into a situation where, as a performer and as a character, he is at his most vulnerable.

The same approach can be seen in, for example, two of the dramatists Albee particularly admires, Chekhov and Beckett. In Act III of *Three Sisters* Chekhov brilliantly contrives that Andrei's confession to his sisters shall take place as extended speech (an aria?) while they are out of sight behind the dressing-screens in the bedroom setting. Beckett in his turn, with his acute sense of medium, obliges his actor in *Krapp's Last Tape* to listen to his own performance on tape, or in *Not I* makes the actress describe in a febrile monologue the situation in which she actually finds herself, while denying that she refers to herself at all. This vulnerability connects with Albee's major themes: he depends upon his performers to register the absence of crucial values in the imaginative world of the play. It is clear that an actor finds it much easier to focus on concrete issues. When Albee directed the 1976 revival of *Who's Afraid of Virginia Woolf?* he encountered particular difficulty in the reaction of Colleen Dewhurst and Ben Gazzara to the fantasy child: Albee asked his performers to remain players in his game and not to lose themselves in the simple imaginative conviction of the dead child. For this he needed actors who were prepared to play when certainty was removed. Dramatically it is vital to the play that we experience the struggle of George and Martha as being concerned with dreadful absences in their lives. On the other hand, to produce this experience places an unusual demand on the performers.

The crises of other plays depend on the performers'

ability to respond to absence and loss, generalised sensations which for many actors might seem too nebulous as a basis for their imaginative work. Harry and Edna's fear of 'nothing' in *A Delicate Balance* is the most evident case, and it is carefully written and notated for performance. Its effect depends entirely on the sensitivity of the performers to the ideas of isolation which inspire Albee. In *All Over* the conception of the play involves the virtual absence of the dying man from the action of the play, although he lies in the up-stage death bed, and for all but one of the family group he signifies values they never encountered. In *The Lady from Dubuque* the elements which Albee described as 'hallucinatory' revolve around the mother figure, who is again absent and is played by Elizabeth in the second act.

The sensation of absence necessarily produces demands which exacerbate the strain of performance, not surprising in a writer who thinks in terms of the tension of performance, whether this is produced from the drama, or from the type of theatrical situation in which the performance is placed. Irene Worth described the problem in the case of the prayer she had to deliver in *Tiny Alice*.

It's the most difficult thing I've ever done. It's so abstract, and I have to define it on three levels – the general fear of being consumed by fire, the specific fear of giving in to a part of my nature and falling in love with Julian, and the religious urge to re-dedicate myself to Alice.[27]

On the other hand, Albee provides his actors with a rhythmic text which is the real basis of the performance. Amid all the difficulties of the production of *Tiny Alice* Gielgud paid tribute to Albee's use of language. While he refused to the last to play the entire closing speech of

Julian, as being too lengthy, he admired the rhythm and music of the writing. Albee's text allows the implied absence to be experienced by performer and audience: it is given little explicit discussion. In this way much of his writing develops the significance of the empty photograph frames in *The Zoo Story*:

> PETER: It doesn't sound a very nice place . . . where you live.
>
> GERRY: Well, no; it isn't an apartment in the East Seventies. But then again, I don't have one wife, two daughters, two cats and two parakeets. What I do have, I have toilet articles, a few clothes, a hot plate that I'm not supposed to have, a can opener, one that works with a key, you know; a knife, two forks, and two spoons, one small, one large; three plates, a cup, a saucer, a drinking glass, two picture frames, both empty, eight or nine books, a pack of pornographic playing-cards, regular deck, an old Western Union typewriter that prints nothing but capital letters . . .
>
> PETER: (*stares glumly at his shoes, then*): About those two empty picture frames . . .?
>
> JERRY: I don't see why they need any explanation at all. Isn't it clear? I don't have pictures of anyone to put in them.

Lately, Albee has demonstrated more clearly his interest in the performer as distinct from the character he assumes. In *Counting the Ways* he requires the actor and actress to 'reveal themselves'. They move out of character and confront the audience with an improvised statement about themselves, before going on with the next vaudeville scene. The device makes both audience and performer acutely aware of the risks which theatrical performance involves.

In a similar way the performers in *The Lady from Dubuque* occasionally break from the natural pattern of the dialogue and comment directly to the audience on the action of the play. The technique breaks into the apparent naturalism of the play and exposes the artifice of the stage. The attention that the actor accepts in inviting the audience to join in a different relationship with the stage is the source of a special tension and energy which is then part of the rhythm of the play overall.

Albee has not discussed the demands he makes on performers to any great extent. At one point he was obliged to reply to criticism that he used English performers in his *Tiny Alice*: 'When we began to look for performers we discovered there were virtually no American actors available who could speak the kind of language that is in this play, which is a rather sorry comment on the state of acting in this country today.'[28] Over the years Albee has cast his plays from a restricted number of actors, showing his confidence in their technical abilities, and has derived a certain freedom to experiment in key respects.

Very early in his career, while discussing publicly the importance of musical ideas to his method, Albee confessed the difficulty of explaining what this meant in practical terms. Nevertheless the idea is Albee's own and helps explain the way he prepares a script for performance. Characters imagined as if with a life of their own are not apparently *musical* creations. On one level he creates the illusion of characters like those of real life. However, the processes whereby the illusion is created can have as much to do with the composition of performance scores as with the intuitive rendering of images of life on the stage.

The comparison with Strindberg's chamber theatre grows closer at this point. Strindberg too described the musical aspect of performance and pointed out how in his

Intimate Theatre with its 150 seats the mannered performance of the larger theatres would seem false and unconvincing. In the small auditorium the virtue of naturalness would be apparent, and above all the vocal qualities of the performance would affect an audience. Strindberg therefore suggests that the actor should adopt the methods of the singer: 'piano and forte . . . crescendo and diminuendo . . . accelerando and ritardando. (The actor should know these musical terms and have them constantly in mind, because they say almost everything.)'[29]

Albee similarly thinks of the control which is possible in musical composition and performance:

> You notate a play like a piece of music. By the use of punctuation, emphasis, underlining, you indicate the way a line is to be spoken. Two or three people in conversation are like two or three instruments answering each other. The structure of drama is similar to musical structure. When you have a dramatist who writes as precisely as Chekhov or Beckett, you can actually conduct the play – you know there is a silence here, a phrase there. . . .[30]

The introduction to *Box* and *Quotations from Chairman Mao* makes clear how important and exact his use of punctuation is. In the plays which followed, the economy of the sentence structure and the precision of the punctuation notate the rhythms. In this example from *Counting the Ways* Albee uses careful punctuation to hold together an extended reflection on the past – part narrative, part description:

> Hm! And I was at a dance, and we all wore satin then and looked very much alike – not from the satin, not only

that, but our hair was of a style, and our skin – what was it? Was it something we used, or was it seventeen? – our skin was glistening and palest pink – save when we blushed, which was deep and often – the palest pink, and we all had a bit of . . . pudge. That's a nice way to put it, I think: a bit of pudge. I had come, I think, with the boy my mother said I should, and that didn't matter, for one was like another. I think I was *sixteen*. One was like another: one bit his nails; one wore brown shoes, dirty brown shoes with his tux; another . . . these roses will wilt. Ah, well.

One was like another and it didn't matter. The music was . . . well, it was a prom.

The other avenue open to Albee in shaping the performance is his highly individual use of stage directions. Apart from being the means of scoring and clarifying the actions, these are used as an indication of the sort of vocal gesture Albee requires. This is an equivalent of the musical expression mark, one indication which characterises the dramatic aspects of the musical performance. As Albee's writing develops he is increasingly economical in his indications, summing up a mood in a word – 'triste' becomes a favourite. While indicating the precise action to be played, the directions give the performer an idea of the sound and rhythm of the words. The following extract from *A Delicate Balance* shows this use prominently:

> AGNES (*an overly sweet smile*): Claire could tell us so much if she cared to, could you not, Claire. Claire who watches us from the sidelines, has seen so very much, has seen us all so clearly, have you not Claire. You were named for nothing.
> CLAIRE (*a pleasant warning*): Lay off, Sis.

AGNES: (*eyes level on* EDNA *and* HARRY; *precisely and not too nicely*): What do you *want*?

HARRY: (*after a pause and a look at* EDNA): I don't know what you mean.

EDNA: (*seemingly puzzled*): Yes.

AGNES: (*eyes narrow*): What do you *really . . . want?*

Stage directions and punctuation combine to guide the actors' delivery of the line and conception of the action. This is an efficient use of the dramatist's resources; it becomes vital when the performance depends upon the realisation of the physical values of language.

From time to time Albee's musical ear is evident in a similar attention which his characters give to words spoken on the stage:

EDGAR: Do what Fred says, huhh?

(*To* FRED *and* CAROL) That's swell, kids; that is just swell.

OSCAR (*to the audience*): I haven't heard 'swell' in a very long time. Can you remember when you last heard 'swell'? (*The Lady from Dubuque*)

This foregrounding of language lies behind the pastiche and parody which is frequently to be found in Albee's writing. In *The Zoo Story* Jerry's speeches are full of irony, often developed in mock-biblical language:

The poor animal gobbled the food down as usual, smiled, which almost made me sick, and then, BAM. But, I sprinted up the stairs, as usual, and the dog didn't get me as usual. AND IT CAME TO PASS THAT THE BEAST WAS DEATHLY ILL. I knew this because he no longer attended me, and because the landlady sobered up. She stopped

me in the hall the same evening of the attempted murder
and confided the information that God had struck her
puppydog a surely fatal blow.

Albee's achievement in the story of Jerry and the Dog is
against the odds. He inserts a set piece which is fully one
third of the length of the printed text, and in which his
second actor is quite passive – the stage direction requiring
him eventually to be 'hypnotized'. This narrative, which is
the real 'Zoo Story', is raised by stages from the level of a
park-bench conversation to an extended parable which
explains the religious imagery of the conclusion. The
suggestion of Jerry's disturbed character is increased by the
ironical speech which conceals the emotional realities of
the role. There is no contradiction between the parody in
the style and the agonised irony which underlies it. The
language is highly artificial and calculated, but sounds
flippant and defensive: 'At any rate, and you've missed the
eight-thousand-dollar question, Peter; at any rate, the dog
recovered his health and the landlady recovered her thirst,
in no way altered by the bow-wow's deliverance.' The style
of language introduces the symbolism of the tale without
affecting the natural social encounter. The idea of the
landlady and dog as a modern-day Charon and Cerberus is
perhaps part of Gerry's spoof delivery – 'she and the dog
are the gatekeepers of my dwelling' – but also there is the
clear possibility that, like Tennessee Williams, whose
Orpheus Descending was performed in 1957 in New York,
Albee is drawing on the Orphic myth of redemption. The
lightness of his touch dismisses the classical and biblical
interpretations in the self-parody of the character.

This feeling for language involves a search for expression
which makes the idiom appear in plays where the setting
and characters are familiar. Not only does Albee give the

actors good text to perform; he gives them carefully conceived things to say. The result has been that his language and his theatre has appeared increasingly calculated, and to many, cold. Albee has long seen this problem: 'What bothers people is the way my characters talk. They tend to be articulate. I don't understand why some think my plays are cold and intellectual.'[31] The more authoritatively Albee approaches his medium, the less his audience seems prepared to encounter and explore his experiments. The plays are as passionate as they ever were but the writer is as intensely committed to his dramatic method as he is to his subjects.

4
'Who's Afraid of Virginia Woolf?'

Who's Afraid of Virginia Woolf? transformed Albee overnight from an off-Broadway experimenter into an American classic. The play was performed on Broadway: Albee's producers and associates Richard Barr and Clinton Wilder showed unusual confidence in ensuring this, even though, equally unusually, they managed to mount the production for about half the cost of the standard straight play. It ran at the Billy Rose Theatre for two years, receiving two awards as the best play of the 1962–3 season, and earning the dramatist an instant reputation. A comparison with Eugene O'Neill imposed itself, both in terms of the perennial search for the successor to the pioneer of modern American drama, and also in recognition of the power and the very length of the play. The pundits were not slow to retitle it: Long Night's Journey into Day – or daze, seeing the resemblance to O'Neill's great autobiographical work; while others, more impressed by what they regarded as a sex battle in the play, likened Albee to Strindberg. The comparisons did not flatter the young playwright. His achievement in sustaining his quartet of players through an action of such length and intensity is remarkable.

Albee seemed to have no difficulty in moving from the small-scale works to the creation of a full-length, three-act form. His preferred subjects plainly had the potential for a more extended treatment, but his success in developing them would depend on his control of form. More of the same was not the answer. The brevity of *The Zoo Story* eases the difficulty of finding a form which conveys by implication the significant absence of values that is its guiding idea. For Albee to succeed he has to create a texture of action and reaction, and at the same time inform it with the capacity to suggest moral and emotional incompleteness. The one-act plays achieve this in more obvious ways, by satire and criticism often contained in disturbingly violent images, which can then be represented as expressions of weakness, isolation or moral poverty. To take this to the length of three acts required a new sophistication of form, so that the sensual awareness the audience has of the action is complemented by its intellectual perception of its potential significance, giving a momentum and logic to such a sustained involvement.

In *Who's Afraid of Virginia Woolf?* Albee balances the roles so that the audience's involvement with the narrative of the play and the destinies of the characters produces a tension between conflicting sympathies and expectations; but in addition he forms the play so that, as the audience responds, there is a sequence of natural interpretation and reinterpretation which does not cohere in expected ways. The *dissatisfaction* of expectations paradoxically allows him to resolve the violent interaction of his characters. The combination of unusual sensations of breakdown and the massive emotional flow of the play consort to make the climax of the play the most moving that Albee has yet achieved.

The action of the play is very simple in outline. After a party on the campus of a small college in New England, ominously named New Carthage to suggest impending destruction, George, a history professor, and Martha, his wife and daughter of the college principal, entertain a bright newcomer, Nick, a biology instructor, and his mousy wife, Honey. As the liquor flows and party games are invented, a crisis results in which the nature of the two relationships is recognisable. Nick discloses to George that he married Honey only after he knew of a pregnancy which was later found to be hysterical. While Honey and Nick are childless, George and Martha have a son, first mentioned fleetingly by Martha and increasingly presented as a source of anger and tension between the characters. The stories of family life have a capacity to damage the participants in the telling. If nothing else, and there is much more, each couple have a secret truth to their relationship which they are unwilling to face, and which despite them emerges in the course of the play.

Story-telling is fundamental to Albee's method. He uses it to challenge the way an audience makes meanings, and its prejudice in favour of the forms of everyday reality. The style of this play appears to encourage the illusion of naturalistic character with a detailed and fixed life history. Hence stories will be 'true' or 'false'. Nick and Honey's union is based on events which Nick drunkenly confides to George in the second act. Albee has confirmed that he intended alcohol to alter the viewpoints of his characters, and here we see it. As George pumps Nick for information, the facts begin to merge with imagination:

NICK: . . . It was a hysterical pregnancy. She blew up, and then she went down.

GEORGE: And while she was up, you married her.

NICK: And then she went down.

They both laugh, and are a little surprised that they do.

The details of a life and a marriage are smothered here in the swapping of boozy tales between the drunken men. George reduces still further the dignity of the exchange by guessing that money entered into the picture:

NICK: You see . . .

GEORGE: There were other things.

NICK: Yes.

GEORGE: To compensate.

NICK: Yes.

GEORGE: There always are.

Albee shows how stories can be twisted and angled. George will change direction at will: he compares Martha with Honey, who got her money from her preacher father, asserting that in both cases the money is embezzled. Following Nick's objection George tells another story, of how Martha's money came from a stepmother. Together the two men turn the narration into a burlesque fairytale: 'Martha's father's second wife was a very old lady with warts who was very rich . . . a witch . . . who married the white mouse.' Nick is 'quite beside himself' as he casts his own father-in-law in the story too, as a 'church mouse'. The importance of the stories goes far beyond the uneasy sharing of confidence and the betrayal to which this will lead when George takes his revenge on the guests at the end of the second act. Although the revelation of the 'truth' of the stories has an obvious impact, the ambiguities of the various accounts creates a disturbing effect. Albee repeatedly destabilises the dramatic balance as he moves towards the striking *coup de théâtre* when it is revealed finally that Martha and George's child does not exist. While Nick hangs on to the facts, George casts doubt on the stories they have shared

> NICK: . . . Your wife never mentioned a stepmother.
>
> GEORGE (*considers it*): Well . . . maybe it isn't true.
>
> NICK (*narrowing his eyes*): And maybe it is.
>
> GEORGE: Might be . . . might not. Well, I think your storey's a lot nicer . . . about your pumped-up little wife, and your father-in-law who was a priest . . .
>
> NICK: He was not a priest . . . he was a man of God.

The underlying tensions of the play are established initially in the opening skirmishes of Act I – titled 'Fun and Games' – where the tone changes as George insists that Martha not 'start in on the bit about the kid'. Her reaction is to threaten her husband at the crucial moments where the guests are waiting at the door and, slightly later, when she drags Honey upstairs. Not only does Martha mention the child to Honey but she also delays returning to the stage. She is changing her dress. Both facts are innocently reported by Honey and greeted with ominous fury by George as the first moves in a destructive process which will transform the 'Fun and Games' of the first act into the 'Walpurgisnacht' of the second before the 'Exorcism' of the third is possible.

The implications of events are felt in the game-playing. Details assume a value dependent on the rules of the game, known only to the hosts. At one stage George cryptically moves his conversation with Nick to some wider political attack. The idea of the sacrifice of a young American

generation is ruminated and then rejected and replaced
with another ploy.

> GEORGE: Not one son-of-a-bitch got killed. Of course,
> nobody bombed Washington. No . . . that's not fair.
> You have any kids?
> NICK: Uh . . . no . . . not yet. (*Pause*) You?
> GEORGE (*a kind of challenge*): That's for me to know and
> you to find out.

This sort of innuendo is characteristic of the play, where,
whatever the exchange, the values which lie beneath the
surface of the action are constantly being stirred and are
giving energy to the performance. The overt aggression
with which Martha treats George is exciting and intriguing
because of the sense of game it conveys. Act I concludes
ferociously as Martha attacks George for his failure as
heir-apparent to her father, accusing him of being a 'great
. . . big . . . fat . . . flop'; 'almost in tears', he smashes the
bottle he is holding and begs her to stop. As she continues
he pleads with her and then drowns her voice by singing
'Who's afraid of Virginia Woolf?' Martha's 'viciously
triumphant' assault is brought to an end by George's
refusal to play that game to a conclusion. Similarly, when
Martha's blatant advances to Nick culminate in her inviting
him upstairs in George's full hearing, there is an
extraordinary strain in the disgusting games that are being
played. The meaning of what is happening is implicit in
those strains and goes far beyond the superficial invitation
Martha has extended in private to the blond middleweight:

> GEORGE: I'd rather read, Martha, if you don't mind . . .
> MARTHA (*her anger close to tears, her frustration to fury*):
> Well, I do mind. Now you pay attention to me! You
> come off this kick you're on, or I swear to God I'll do

> it. I swear to God I'll follow that guy into the kitchen,
> and then I'll take him upstairs, and . . .
>
> GEORGE (*swinging around to her again . . . loud . . .
> loathing*): SO WHAT, MARTHA?

Despite the appearance of betrayal, Martha's infidelity is
no more than a hopeless move in a struggle which the two of
them have agreed is to be 'total war'. Nick, who believes he
will make his way to the top of the college by 'plowing a few
pertinent wives', fails at Hump-the-Hostess. The games
that are played have all the appearances of a 'marital
corrida', which is how one critic described the play. They
have, however, less to do with the institution of marriage
than with the experience of a complex set of values which is
expressed in the mixture of energy and despair which unite
George and Martha. She destroys him and yet believes that
he can withstand her. Albee seems to be moving in
paradoxes, and often the contradictions of George and
Martha's relationship are used teasingly to engineer games
that the opposition has no chance of winning; but Martha's
elegy for George in the final act shows the paradox to be
essential to the play. Martha explains to Nick that one man
alone has made her happy:

> George, who is out there somewhere in the dark . . .
> George who is good to me, and whom I revile;
> who understands me, and whom I push off;
> who can make me laugh, and I choke it back in my
> throat;
> who can hold me, at night, so that it's warm, and who I
> will bite so there's blood;
> who keeps learning the games we play as quickly as I can
> change the rules; who can make me happy and I do not
> wish to be happy, and yes I do wish to be happy. George
> and Martha: sad, sad, sad.

This strange combination of love and despair and aggression has earned the play high praise, and the attention of critics anxious to attach the moral and emotional experience of the play to interpretations of what the meaning of the dramatist may be. On a number of occasions Albee has confirmed that there is a connection with American politics and history particularly in the struggles of the childless couple:

> There is some notion in my mind, while I was working on the play, and it's not terribly important, but it was there, which is the reason actually that I named the couple George and Martha after General and Mrs Washington. There might be an allegory to be drawn, and have the fantasy child the revolutionary principles of this country that we haven't lived up to yet.[32]

There is no doubt that details in Albee's scheme point to implications wider than any domestic drama. George reads and quotes from a history of Western civilisation; there are references to the stand for Berlin, to China; and in the character of Nick there is the suggestion of Nikita Khrushchev and a new technological society in the East which offers nothing to the declining West. The conflict between George and Nick is at one moment represented as a conflict between two attitudes to the present: George, in history, looks back; Nick, in biology, looks forward. The sterility of the younger couple is set side by side with George's vision of the brave new world of the genetic engineers: 'People do . . . uh . . . have kids. That's what I meant about history. You people are going to make them in test-tubes, aren't you? You biologists. Babies. Then the rest of us . . . them as wants to . . . can screw to their heart's content.' Nick and Honey are childless, and, significantly, Nick's encounter with Martha is a sexual failure.

Despite Albee's clue to the possible meanings of the play his remarks are in no way a key to the text. One has only to consider the life of the play in performance to judge how relatively unimportant are specific interpretative points of this sort, however much we may be interested in the fragments of conscious inspiration that the playwright recalls. They take their place alongside the reminiscences of O'Neill or Williams which the literary sleuth can track down: pointers to the sensitivity of the creative imagination. What is remarkable is how Albee's conscious social and political ideas are worked out in terms of a deeply personal style of expression. The play is both a lament for society and also the expression of personal grief and loss. In a remarkably beautiful speech, a meditation spoken in Act II 'at Nick, not to him', George links art and society in a way which is very close to Albee's stated view:

You take the trouble to construct a civilization . . . to . . . to build a society, based on the principles of . . . of principle . . . you endeavor to make communicable sense out of natural order, morality out of the unnatural disorder of man's mind . . . you make government and art, and realize that they are, must be, both the same . . . you bring things to the saddest of all points . . . to the point where there *is* something to lose . . . then all at once, through all the music, through all the sensible sounds of men building attempting, comes the *Dies Irae*. And what is it? What does the trumpet sound? Up yours.

Albee's use of the fantasy child was most seriously criticised and proved a stumbling-block to the full appreciation of his achievement. On one hand it offered a notion which unified the interpretations of the work; and on the other the child was found to strain the conviction of the audience. With a measure of hindsight, and the development of Albee's style, it can be seen that he was being pressed into a naturalistic and symbolic mould which in a number of crucial ways he does not fit. Accordingly the child was explained in terms of significance, but was felt by many to be an improbable delusion in such a couple as George and Martha. Albee did not accept the resulting criticism, feeling the child was a 'rather important development'.

The understatement is acid. The child is essential. Provoked by Martha's breaking of the rules (not, as has been suggested, by Martha's infidelity), George conceives and plays to a conclusion the destruction of their most sustaining 'game' – the fiction of their child. It is the game in which there can be no third and fourth players, and, when they *are* involved, it is inevitable that George must accept the crisis and play it through. The only role for Nick and Honey is in the funeral rites of Martha's child.

The decision brings all four players to a point where the games are at an end and the reality of their relationships and lives have to be confronted. Albee again explained the play's significance by glossing the title as 'Who's afraid of a life without illisions'. But the discussion can hardly end here. These points are clear and are even parodied within the text when Martha throws off her O'Neill impression:

NICK: You're all crazy: nuts.

MARTHA (*affects a brogue*): Awww, 'tis the refuge we take when the unreality of the world weighs too heavily on our tiny heads. (*Normal voice again*) Relax; sink into it; you're no better than anybody else.

NICK (*wearily*): I think I am.

Who's Afraid of Virginia Woolf?

In performance the questions of reality and unreality and the value of the roles are not so many stages in an argument, but part of a complex experience based in the physical sensations of performance. Thus the absent child is no mere symbol (a much-misused word) but for all four performers the essential condition for a profound emotional encounter. It does not technically matter that the child will turn out to be a fantasy. At the moment of performance it is imagined and given life in the actions of the stage. At the instant of playing it is real enough.

George and Martha's son is the subject of their increasingly ferocious games, but also the element which realises the power of Albee's scheme. For example, when Honey first reveals her knowledge that there is a child, it produces an effect beyond the breaking of a taboo. Nick greets the news triumphantly, recalling the earlier skirmish in which George has challenged him and avoided answering the question whether he has a child or not, and in which George has imagined child-bearing being given over to the laboratory. Honey reacts naïvely and earns George's disproportionate response. The interactions are unnerving in a variety of ways. Albee is not making a point, but exciting performers and audience alike to the sensitive areas of his play:

HONEY (*to* GEORGE, *brightly*): I didn't know until just a minute ago that you had a son.
GEORGE (*wheeling as if struck from behind*): WHAT?
HONEY: A son! I hadn't known.
NICK: You to know and me to find out. Well, he must be quite big . . .
HONEY: Twenty-one . . . twenty-one tomorrow . . . tomorrow's his birthday.
NICK (*a victorious smile*): Well!!

GEORGE (*to* HONEY): She told you about him?
HONEY (*flustered*): Well, *yes*. Well, I mean. . . .
GEORGE (*nailing it down*): She told you about him.
HONEY (*a nervous giggle*): Yes.
GEORGE (*strangely*): You say she's changing?

Albee's stage direction shows the effect he desires. The strangeness of this moment comes from the varied understandings of the situation which are finely established in each role, and the private significance of the child as an image for each player. The viability of the idea lies in this plurality of response, not in the one 'true' version, which is, of course, a disappointment to the spectator who requires an everyday solution to the problems of the play. Honey and Nick's reactions are ultimately expressions of the dehumanised situation in which they, the couple of the American Dream, find themselves. Honey, terrified at the idea of bearing children, secretly avoids conceiving. The actress is given a short sequence at the conclusion of 'Walpurgisnacht' when she emerges from the bathroom 'The worse for wear, half asleep, still sick, still staggering a little . . . in something of a dream world.' She has been woken by George hurling his book at the door-chimes. Honey's dream shows her inability to confront reality: 'there was someone there . . . I was . . . naked . . . NO! . . . I DON'T WANT . . . ANY . . . I DON'T WANT THEM . . . GO 'WAY . . . (*Begins to cry*) I DON'T WANT . . . ANY . . . CHILDREN.'

Following a moment of recognition and compassion, George launches a devastating attack on this quintessential avoidance of life. Honey refuses to listen as he proposes to explain the sounds that can be heard from the couple off-stage. The energy of George's contemptuous dismissal of both himself, the contemplative outsider, and those he observes altering and destroying the future, derives from the image of the child.

> It's very simple . . . When people can't abide things as they are, when they can't abide the present, they do one of two things . . . either they . . . either they turn to a contemplation of the past, as I have done, or they set about to . . . alter the future. And when you want to change something . . . you BANG! BANG! BANG! BANG!
>
> HONEY: Stop it!
> GEORGE: And you, you simpering bitch . . . you don't want *children*?

Honey is a key witness to the moving games which George and Martha play around the theme of the child. Nick registers what is fact, Honey a naïve fear. The two roles supply a range of crude responses to the inventions surrounding George and Martha's child. The announcement of the death gives the tone of the writing. It is crucial that George's role is conscious invention at this point, as this allows the coexistence of wit and emotion seen in the 'strange half smile' Albee requires from the actor.

> HONEY (*so faintly*): I'm going to be sick.
> GEORGE (*turning away from her . . . he, too, softly*): Are you? That's nice.
> (MARTHA's *laugh is heard again.*)
> Oh, listen to that.
> HONEY: I'm going to die.
> GEORGE (*quite beside himself now*): Good . . . good . . . you go right ahead.

(*Very softly, so that* MARTHA *could not possibly hear*)
Martha? Martha? I have some terrible news for you.
(*There is a strange half-smile on his lips.*) It's about our
. . . son. He's dead. Can you hear me Martha? Our boy
is dead.

(*He begins to laugh, very softly . . . it is mixed with
crying.*)

This sort of ambivalence in the playing goes far beyond the
creation of one-off effects of surprise. When Nick in the
final moments claims to 'understand' the pretence, it is
clear he ironically misses the point, while from a totally
different standpoint Honey seems to accept entirely the
rules of the game and joins in the Latin rite for the dead.
For George and Martha the child is a necessity and at the
same time the evidence of their insecurity. He is cherished,
and can be used to whatever ends the domestic battle may
require. Martha can taunt George over the paternity of
child, suggesting a Strindbergian sex contest, and George
counter with a passionately confident statement of belief in
his share in creating his 'blond-eyed, blue-haired . . . son'.

The child is the key to the structure of fictions which
widen the range of the play and which provide the audience
with altering perspectives on the characters. George's story
of the boy he knew at prep school who was humiliated when
he ordered 'bergin' in a speakeasy, and who accidently
killed his mother with a shotgun and his father in a road
accident, becomes the novel which Martha cruelly reveals
her father prevented George publishing and which was his
own story. Events are presented as straight narrative but
reappear transformed. As George later challenges Nick,
'Truth or illusion. Who knows the difference, eh, toots?
Eh?' It can hardly be said to be the case that George killed
his father and mother *and* was committed to a mental

asylum where he has been for thirty years without speaking. The story is still more indeterminate once George has used the details of the road accident to relate to Martha the way her son died. On the other hand the story of the boy in the asylum, out of touch with an unbearable reality, expresses the alienation of George's own experience, where alcohol is a sort of escape similar to a 'needle jammed in the arm'. The reappearance of the details of this story as novel, then 'truth', then manifest invention, indicates how consciously Albee is aiming at undermining the illusion of *fact*, and substituting a shifting, developing *experience* for the audience. The experience is the product of art and the methods of the play frequently come close to making this explicit.

At the moment of George's invention of the son's death, he and Martha superimpose versions of the child's life which are palpable fictions, but Albee is not leading his audience to expect 'facts' at all. The fantasies allow him to get down to the bone and, as George says, beyond, to the marrow. The bare facts are that there is something missing, the fictions create the experience of what it is. 'Bringing up baby' is a game, but also contains passages of compassionate and disturbingly destructive writing. The whole is introduced as a formal part of the play. The stage direction requires 'an almost tearful recitation' and accordingly George coaches Martha in her performance. The obviousness of performance in no way detracts from the impact of Martha's recitation. This is one of those moments where Albee's musical conception of his art is apparent. The evocation of the child is given a counterpoint in the prayer for the absolution of the dead:

MARTHA: . . . And his eyes were green . . . green with . . . if you peered so deep into them . . . so deep . . .

> bronze . . . bronze parentheses around the irises . . .
> such green eyes!
> GEORGE: . . . blue, green, brown . . .
> MARTHA: . . . and he loved the sun! . . . He was tan
> before and after everyone . . . and the sun in his hair
> . . . became . . . fleece.
> GEORGE (*echoing her*): . . . fleece . . .
> MARTHA: . . . beautiful, beautiful boy.
> GEORGE: Absolve, Domine, animas omnium fidelium
> defunctorum ab omni vinculo delictorum.

As a performance score this allows naturalistic 'illusions' to
achieve an altogether deeper level of expression. It is
probable that Albee's first director, Alan Schneider,
allowed the stage presentation to suggest too clearly the
everyday and accordingly he created some uneasiness with
these transformations that occur so freely with the roles.
The range in Martha's account of the child is striking.
'Beautiful; wise; perfect', she says of her son, and justly,
George has the line 'There's a real mother talking.' Albee
intends mockery in the remark, but the impact is precisely
that of a mother. Yet the account of the child is also
extended to express the struggle within a marrage, the child
being the victim of the 'lies' they tell of each other

> GEORGE: . . . She has a son who fought her every inch of
> the way who didn't want to be turned into a weapon
> against his father, who didn't want to be used as a
> goddam club whenever Martha didn't get things like
> she wanted them!
> MARTHA (*rising to it*): Lies! Lies!
> GEORGE: Lies? All right. A son who would *not* disown his
> father, who came to him for advice, for information,
> for love that wasn't mixed with sickness – and you

know what I mean, Martha! – who could not tolerate
the slashing, braying residue that called itself his
MOTHER. MOTHER? HAH!!

When Albee himself directed the 1976 revival of *Who's
Afraid of Virginia Woolf?* this section of the play presented
difficulties for his principal performers, Coleen Dewhurst
and Ben Gazzara. They were looking for a naturalistic basis
for their work, taking the loss of the child too realistically.
Albee's description of the quality of performance he
requires is highly instructive: 'what we were getting was a
kind of dirge-like quality . . . mourning. It was heavy and
yet not really intense. After I explained the child as a kind
of metaphoric game-playing, the dirge-like quality was
gone and they were playing more intensely.'[33]
This most moving section of the play is to be treated as a
game, to be played intensely. The consequence is a frank
opposition of the performers playing one against another
with what is the available material. This is good
fundamental acting technique. If the performer trusts the
quality of action composed by the playwright, the intensity
and conviction will arise from the act of performance. It
cannot be derived from a comprehensive interpretation of
the characters and their backgrounds which precedes the
experience of the play in rehearsal and performance. In this
respect Albee is likely to suffer at the hands of American
actors whose tradition is fundamentally naturalistic and
who look for the precise interpretation of the role in its
social and psychological context. Albee is notable for the
extremly limited number of artists with whom he has
worked and for the exacting demands he makes in the
casting of a play: a necessary conequence of the demands of
his style. *Who's Afraid of Virginia Woolf?* is, however, a
natural vehicle for performers and the best introduction to

Albee's concept of finely controlled action. Uta Hagen and Arthur Hill, the original George and Martha, were instantly struck by the quality of the roles they were offered and recognised their theatrical vitality. They remained with the production from October 1962 to the end of December 1963. There is no report of staleness.

Speaking of his own production, Albee pointed out the quality of his casting lay in strength: 'They're both strong performers – such tough actors – that it's an equal battle. In this play balance is everything.' The quality of the battle is probably what most remember in the film version starring Elizabath Taylor and Richard Burton, which produced their finest collaboration on the screen. Albee had suggested Bette Davis and James Mason for these roles, which would have added spice to Martha's impression of the film star in the opening lines. In the event the pairing of an American and British performance was effectively what Taylor and Burton supplied in terms of style. In addition their personal and professional relationship seemed to fuse to give an ensemble performance of care and understanding as well as the intensity which was expected. Albee himself admired the result.

George and Martha are one of the classic double acts of the modern stage, like Pinter's McCann and Goldberg or Beckett's Vladimir and Estragon. Indeed there are moments in the play when the sheer theatrical vitality of the pairing breaks out, as in the echo of *Waiting for Godot* where George and Martha trade insults: 'Monstre!' 'Cochon!' 'Bête!' 'Canaille!' 'Putain!'; or when they turn their concerted act on Nick:

NICK: I'm nobody's houseboy . . .
GEORGE AND MARTHA: . . . now! (*Sing*) I'm nobody's houseboy now . . . (*Both laugh.*)

76

The balance is required for the game to be played to its harrowing conclusions. Albee's reaction after the New York performance of O'Neill's *The Iceman Cometh* was that, although the playwright made a case for the necessary life-lie in his treatment of the illusions of the clientele of Harry the Hope's bar, he felt that it was best to make the effort to live with truth. His own use of 'illusion' is quite different from O'Neill's. George and Martha's games are not strictly illusions: they are routines with which they fill a life which is intrinsically lacking in the completeness of social and family relationships. The play shows these coexisting with a sensation of the true state of the couple: alone together and threatened by reality.

The final act, 'The Exorcism', produces a catharsis in which the shedding of the last routine reveals the nature of their existence; it has the classic tragic quality of recognition and reversal. The play presents the emotional truth of the character relationship and the moment of a profound change of destiny. Like a classical tragedy the play works towards a catastrophe in which there will be no 'message' affirmed and no superior course of action advocated; but rather the moral values of the characters will be affirmed and the dignity and resource of humanity will be celebrated with an audience made aware of its own circumscribed happiness. In the spectacle of George and Martha's battle the audience does not see merely the violence that at one point so delights Honey, but also the pathos of their relationship and the courage of their insight. They are sustained by games, not illusions. George is or may be an orphan; Martha is discarded by the father she claims to admire: they are in a line of Albee characters who are abandoned and who make something out of the loss.

'The Exorcism' begins with Martha's striking image of the struggle against despair –

> We both cry all the time, and then, what we do, we cry, and take our tears, and we put 'em in the ice box, in the goddam ice trays (*begins to laugh*) until they're all frozen (*laughs even more*) and then . . . we put them . . . in our . . . drinks. (*More laughter, which is something else too.*)

– and concludes with the most simple and naturalistic contemplation of a future unsustained by pretence. Albee explained that he had retitled his play, originally to be called 'The Exorcism', after seeing the words 'Who's Afraid of Virginia Woolf?' scrawled on a mirror in a Greenwich Village bar. Its significance, he stated, might be seen as 'Who's afraid of a life without illusions?' As the concluding tableau of the play confirms, Albee's roles do express such a fear. The massive achievement of his play is that the fear is not disguised, but transformed within the complex roles into an expressive but ultimately unwinnable game.

5
'A Delicate Balance'

A Delicate Balance is a remarkably clear and deft piece of work, and these qualities may have accounted for its qualified success in New York in 1966. *Who's Afraid of Virginia Woolf?* and the 1963 adaptation of Carson McCullers's *The Ballad of the Sad Café* seemed to confirm the dramatist as a specialist in the grotesque. His plays were varied in style but showed the same tendency to push the subject to the limits. 'Sensational' was the word most frequently used in the press to describe Albee in those years, and also describes how people viewed the content of his theatre. Even the obscurities of *Tiny Alice* did not prevent its theatricality from being appreciated.

In contrast *A Delicate Balance* came as an understatement. What, then, were the characteristics of the 'new' Albee? The outstanding impression made by *A Delicate Balance* is one of coolness. The language Albee was working towards in *Tiny Alice* is matched to a simpler visual style – in fact, a return to the deceptive suburban realism of *Who's Afraid of Virginia Woolf?* The effect is less freely naturalistic than in the latter and less spectacular than in the former, producing an impression of control in all dimensions of the medium. As a consequence it may not at first sight appear how condensed and expressive Albee's method is. His style allows the structure of the play to be more carefully arranged. This care is necessary if speech is to achieve the significance within the action that Albee intends. It is characteristic for Albee to place a sensitive area at the heart of the work, and in this play the way in which he approaches the recognition and the definition of the central concern is meticulously controlled through a disciplined, highly articulate prose. At the same time he aims at the suggestion of enigmatic forces which will progressively be translated into action and revealed to the audience.

The action presents a series of critical events in the life of a comfortable middle-aged couple, Agnes and Tobias. The scene is 'the living-room of a large well-appointed suburban house. Now.' The apparent stability and success of the couple's retirement is eroded from the opening lines of the play, and this erosion is a basic process Albee develops. Agnes is taken with the fancy that some day she will lose her mind. The comfortable scene is a delicate balance which can apparently be disturbed. Agnes's sister shares the house and has tipped into a state which parallels madness. For Claire there is no further balance to her life and she takes refuge from its realities in alcohol. She is not an alcoholic, she says, for her drinking is wilful and a deliberate evasion. The two sisters suggest that some disturbing reality underlies the apparent ease and contentment of the scene.

The arrival in successive acts of their daughter Julia and of their 'best friends' Harry and Edna provokes the collapse of the balance which Tobias and Agnes sustain.

A Delicate Balance

The new arrivals establish the relationships of family and friendship, and place demands on the couple. Harry and Edna come because they are alone and fear the emptiness deriving from isolation in a seemingly neighbourly society. Julia returns to her parents each time she fails to establish a lasting marriage. The uninvited guests demonstrate the breakdown of family and friendship in a wider context.

The plotting of *A Delicate Balance* develops the progress of the claims made upon Tobias and Agnes. Their home has not the emotional or moral resources to withstand the demands. It is balanced too precariously, and its energies are directed solely to preserving its own limited stability. Moreover, Albee has the claims of friendship and family conflict and suggests that neither rests upon a secure moral base. Quite simply Albee's play is a battle for the home. Julia wishes to reoccupy her childhood room, which has effectively been commandeered by her parents' friends. There is a strange, violent core to the battle: Agnes and Tobias initially treat it with conventional decorum; Claire cynically sees the primitive aspect as a struggle for a place 'in the cave'. Questions abound. Why the virulence of the fight, why the 'disease' (so-called), why the irrational fear of the outside? Why the moral weakness of Tobias? The collapse of the fragile relationships and the rise of conflict brings him to the point where he must acknowledge the reality of his position: he has no love for his friends. But he has a choice and can affirm their right to stay.

The play is coldly realistic. Albee carefully blends the demands of individuals with the poverty of relationships. A key element in Tobias's position at the conclusion of the play is the recognition that his weakness in some way derives from his inability to survive the death of his son Teddy years before. In refusing to have another child he turned his back on Agnes and reduced his family life to a cipher. It is not hard to recognise a similarity between this action and that of *Who's Afraid of Virginia Woolf?*, where similarly an absent child is used to involve the audience in the spectacle of a couple's painful isolation. That play, however, works largely in retrospect, as the stories of the two couples are unearthed in the 'Fun and Games' of the all-night party. *A Delicate Balance* also has a climax at which a secret loss is revealed, but the action is designed to enlarge the issues of commitment and responsibility and make them fully dramatic.

A certain similarity in form to *Who's Afraid of Virginia Woolf?* should be mentioned. It may in turn be a debt to the later plays of Strindberg, or a reflection of the Christian images which occupy the recesses of Albee's mind. *A Delicate Balance* has the acts arranged in a Passion sequence of Friday, Saturday and Sunday morning. Without overstating the signficance of the arrangement of Passion, Descent into Hell, and Resurrection, one can see that it has, like the 'Walpurgisnacht' of the earlier play, a strongly felt effect in the play. One can follow the sequence from the crisis on Friday, when Harry and Edna bring 'their terror' to the house, through the havoc when Julia returns, to the dawn of Sunday morning and the new clarity with which the household faces life.

In *A Delicate Balance* Albee gets to grips with the relationships of contemporary American society and its family. (In the earlier plays the family had appeared in the simplifying distortions of his absurdist work, or on the periphery of the lives of Jerry, or George and Martha.) This is a step forward in dramatising his sense of personal loss. He creates action as a means of evoking what is not there, and such an approach naturally leads to the shorter and smaller-cast plays. Here he writes for the actual, and not the potential, family relationship; for the group of friends, not the accidental encounter with newcomers or even strangers. This brings Albee into a closer relationship with the everyday rituals of life which he has to weave into the fabric of the play. If these are to be undermined he has to do it with skill.

The opening moments of the play suggest how powerful his method will be. In the luxurious setting Tobias and Agnes share a drink. The initial stage directions give the comfortable mood: Agnes 'speaks usually softly, with a hint of a smile on her face: not sardonic, nor sad . . . wistful, maybe . . .'; Tobias 'speaks somewhat the same way'; Agnes utters 'a small happy laugh'. Social ease is counterpointed with a sense of disturbance. The counterpoint technique is clearly visible in Albee's economical use of the actors' resources. The offering and choice of drinks is counterpointed by the cryptic discussion of madness and the family circle.

> TOBIAS: We will go mad before you. The anisette.
> AGNES (*a small happy laugh*): Thank you, darling. But I could never do it – go adrift – for what would become of you? Still, what I find most astonishing, aside, as I have said, from that speculation – and I wonder too, sometimes, if I am the only one of you to admit to it; not that I may go mad, but that each of you wonders if each of *you* might not – why on earth do you want anisette?
> TOBIAS (*considers*): I thought it might be nice.
> AGNES (*wrinkles her nose*): Sticky . . .

The background physical activity supplies the means for the performer to assimilate to the stage environment, while the real action – the testing of Tobias – goes on. On paper the actress seems to have an impossible task, juggling with three different threads: madness, Julia, and Tobias's defence of Claire. In effect the opening three or four minutes of the play are an extended series of parentheses whereby the intention of the actress is sustained against the unremarkable detail of the family scene. The actress accepts the deflection but returns naturally and insistently to 'the reflex defence of Claire'. The scene is an excellent example of Albee's quasi-musical skill in counterpointing the subtextual level of the actor's intention with the apparent physical level of actions and the stage environment. Once the comfortable surface suggests cracks, the audience is drawn into an active interpretation of events. The opening scene is felt as a balancing-act, and questions arise as to the pressures: why does Tobias defend Claire? And why not? And what is the connection with Agnes's speculation about madness?

The talk of balance and sanity is connected with Albee's recurrent theme of the threat posed by reality. With the entrance of Claire an important parallel is established in the two sisters' response to reality. Agnes first alludes to the desirability of an escape from sanity. For her madness would be peace, 'unlike our dear Claire' who seeks relief in alcohol. Claire herself is given (with evident author's wit) exactly the same jokes about Tobias's anisette. She, of course, drinks brandy like her sister. Claire, like Agnes, sees clearly, but she seeks relief at the bottom of a glass. She is to a degree the drunken bum who is the seer of the play. However, while she chides others for their little evasions and deceits, she has herself lost all ability to cope with reality. Agnes with her 'mountain of burdens' maintains the daily struggle while evidently not confronting directly the problems which beset the family.

The overall effect of the play depends on the way in which the avoidance of problems is apprehended by the

1. *The Sandbox* at The Jazz Gallery, NYC, 1961.

2. The 1961 production of *The American Dream* directed by Alan Schneider at The York Playhouse with Ben Piazza and Susie Bond.

3. Alan Schneider's 1961 Broadway production of *Who's Afraid of Virginia Woolf?* with Arthur Hill and Uta Hagen.

4. The final *pietà* from *Tiny Alice* in 1964, with Irene Worth and John Gielgud.

5. *A Delicate Balance* at the Martin Beck Theatre, NYC, in 1966. Performers (l. to r.) are Jessica Tandy, Rosemary Murphy, Carmen Matthews, Hume Cronyn, and Henderson Forsythe.

6. Jessica Tandy as The Wife in *All Over* with Betty Fields and Neil Fitzgerald (Martin Beck Theatre 1971).

8. Frances Conroy and Jo Musante in *The Lady from Dubuque* directed by Alan Schneider in 1980.

7. Fred Voelpel's costumes for Albee's 1975 production of *Seascape* at the Sam S. Shubert Theatre, NYC.

audience naturally and not forced upon them as an issue. The experience of the tensions and moral dilemmas which are Albee's subject is not sacrificed by turning them into philosophical abstractions; important suggestions are made in the most fragmentary fashion. Sometimes the warmth of a moment is accompanied by a suggestion of circumstances we do not understand, as when Agnes says, 'I'm as young as the day I married you – though I'm certain I don't look it – because you're a very good husband . . . most of the time.' This detail is answered by a hint later in Claire's condemnation of Tobias and his circle of friends. Inquiring what he has in common with them, even with Harry, his 'best friend . . . in all the world', she reduces their similarity to the fact that Tobias was, like Harry, *not* a good husband all the time: 'What do you really have in common with your very best friend . . . 'cept the coincidence of having cheated with the same woman . . . girl . . . woman? What except that? And hardly a distinction. I believe she was upended that whole July'.

The suggestion of secrets is vital to Albee's method. Claire reveals the sins of that July, as well as being credited with a deeper level of perception. Beyond this lies the unresolved question of her relationship, raised by Agnes. Was *Claire* the girl that July? The implication is reinforced by her role as *alter ego* to Agnes. Where Agnes is restrained, Claire is drunkenly extrovert. Where Agnes is at the centre of the family, Claire is at its limit. Despite a certain danger of abstraction as clear sight personified, the role is an integral part of the conflicts of the play and supplies an important dimension to the available staging of the various crises in the action. Agnes appears to cope and attempts to preserve the dignity of the family; Claire disgraces the family, and her wilful drinking confirms her defeat by life. Thus her antics with the accordion in II. ii are both infantile and an avoidance of a crisis she understands too well. Her response to reality is also perhaps the key to the strange pantomime where she stretches full length on the floor with her brandy glass on her forehead. Her wisdom and balance are only possible in association with liquor.

Tobias is the central figure in the triptych. The action of the play concerns the way in which this precariously stable arrangement will respond to the intrusion of outside forces, and in particular how the man will respond. Albee subtly suggests that Tobias fails to recognise the pressures:

> CLAIRE: Is Julia having another divorce?
> TOBIAS: Hell, I don't know.
> CLAIRE (*takes glass*): It's only your daughter. Thank you. I should imagine from all that I have . . . watched, that it is come-home time.

When in Act II Julia does appear, Agnes has to insist on the effect that is made to maintain a balance while the others 'teeter, unconcerned or uncaring'. Julia's unhappiness is a burden, and it is implicitly a comparison with the apparent success of her parents. While Julia has divorces 'for all', this exposes the hidden strains which all but Agnes avoid. When Agnes insists on preserving the social graces, it is because they play a part in survival. She sees the situation objectively while she participates in it, even to the extent of suggesting jokingly that she too might, like Julia, have a divorce. Underneath the façade she constructs she coolly admits to 'the gradual demise of intensity, the private preoccupations, the substitutions' encountered in her marriage. Not only is Tobias fundamentally estranged from Agnes; she accuses him of being distant from his daughter. Agnes associates Tobias with the failure of Julia's marriages. Claire is at hand to echo the reproach:

AGNES: If you had talked to Tom or Charlie, yes! even Charlie or . . . uh . . .

CLAIRE: Phil?

AGNES (*no recognition of Claire having helped her*): . . . Phil, it might have done some good. If you decided to assert yourself, finally, too late, I imagine . . .

CLAIRE: Damned if you do, damned it you don't.

AGNES: Julia might, at the very least, come to think her father cares, and that might be a consolidation if not a help.

Agnes and Tobias are in the line of Albee's Mommy and Daddy figures: she gracefully dominant – a 'martinet', is her word – and he hesitant and ineffective. For the first time, however, Albee completes his dramatisation of the family, establishing a role for the child and depicting the family in its wider social setting. The social setting is first established with the arrival on a pleasant Friday evening of the 'best friend . . . in all the world', Harry, together with his wife, Edna.

This utterly normal moment has an electrifying effect. The actor and actress arrive with a clear and urgent intention: to escape the isolation which threatens them. This supplies the subtext to their conventional visit, creating powerful tensions under the forms of ordinary life:

HARRY: So we were sitting, and Edna was doing that – that panel she works on . . .

EDNA (*wistful, some loss*): . . . my needlepoint . . .

HARRY: . . . and I was reading my French; I've got it pretty good now – not the accent, but the . . . words. *A brief silence.*

CLARE (*quietly*): And then?

HARRY (*looks over to her, a little dreamlike, as if he didn't know where he was*): Hmm?

CLAIRE (*nicely*): And then?

HARRY (*looks at* EDNA): I . . . I don't know what happened then; we . . . we were . . . it was all very quiet, and we were all alone . . .

    (EDNA *begins to weep, quietly:* AGNES *notices, the others do not;* AGNES *does nothing.*)

. . . and then . . . nothing happened, but . . .

EDNA (*open weeping, loud*): WE GOT . . . FRIGHTENED.

    (*Open sobbing; no one moves.*)

HARRY (*quiet wonder, confusion*): We got scared.

Harry and Edna, engaged as they are in an evening in early retirement which, in Claire's phrase, would be 'indistinguishable [from] if not necessarily similar' to the evening we see Tobias and Agnes enjoying at the opening of the play, become aware that there is nothing and they are frightened. The scene is carefully constructed to allow the silences to make their effect, with only Claire inviting the couple to tell their story. Agnes, significantly, notices Edna's distress and fails to respond. As Albee constructs the narrative explaining the threat of the absence of value in a life, he dramatises a scene of empty friendship, in which the first gesture is avoidance. When Edna surprises her hosts by asking if she may now go to bed, Agnes is 'distant' and Tobias replies to his friends 'by rote'.

This is the point where Albee ends his first act. The implications are dawning on the audience. The texture of events is best understood in terms of what is *not* there. He has constructed the appearances and gestures which suggest that there is more and less than what we see; and he has articulated the problem of the purposelessness of an existence which, in material terms, is so substantial. Moreover, he has suggested a characteristic of the void which threatens Harry and Edna; for they instinctively seek escape in friendship. This is the appeal to Tobias.

With the return of Julia there is a similarly childlike appeal for love and community and the two are designed to conflict, placing family and friendship at odds. Neither claim is firmly founded. Harry and Edna, like children, want 'comfort'. Claire, standing outside the fray, explains to Julia that their need is like hers: 'Warmth. A special room with a night light, or the door ajar so you can look down the hall from the bed and see that Mommy's door is open.' They want – that is, 'lack' and 'wish for' – love. Julia similarly 'wants' that love and protection. Moreover, she demands it as a matter of right and possession. And underlying it all is the insinuation which Albee has built into the play: love has gone out of the house.

JULIA (*quiet despair*): This is my home!
CLAIRE: This . . . ramble? Yes?

(*Surprised delight*) You're laying claim to the cave! Well I don't know how they'll take to that. We're not a communal nation, dear; giving, but not sharing, outgoing, but not friendly.

Claire penetrates to the bone, coming to the conclusions which are permitted by her own declared inertia. She has no choices to make and is preoccupied by her cynicism and self-disgust, qualities which make perception the easier. The same aspect of human behaviour appealed to Albee in creating the role of Martha. In *A Delicate Balance* the destructive power of Claire's observations are not associated with any initiative. Agnes claims to participate; Claire stands outside. Both are aware of the balance of the situation: it is for Tobias to act. The play organises the claims of family and society into a pressure brought to bear on one man: 'Poor Tobias, surrounded by his women.' Albee likes to put America to the test in the shape of its men.

The crisis of claim and counterclaim is deepened by Albee's ingenious use of the symmetry of the two couples. When Harry and Edna settle, they begin to assume the functions, and even the identities, of their hosts. This disturbing process is unexplained and inevitably alerts the audience to the issue of rights. When Julia breaks down and threatens to shoot the intruders it is in defence of her rights as the daughter of the house. Edna counters with the 'rights' of best friends and godparents. Julia insists with fury that they are guests in the house; therefore they have a circumscribed role, and limited rights. Edna is unmoved by Julia's emotion (a detached effect which is highly effective in performance) and suggests that Julia has another contact with others. She implies the existence of responsibilities 'for quite a few people . . . whose lives are . . . moved – if not necessarily touched' by her actions. The insidious usurpation provokes recognition: the outsiders cannot be ignored. Albee makes certain of the effect by ignoring the process of their assimilation; they simply belong and play the roles which impinge on the security of Tobias's home. They are both the Harry and Edna who lock themselves in their room (Julia's room) in terror, and uncomfortable companions who retain their ease and are even sharply aggressive when their position is challenged. Once established in the house their fear, the 'disease' (dis-ease) Tobias recognises infects the group. Harry and Edna take over the roles to which their similarity entitles them, as the image of their hosts: Agnes asks Harry for a drink since he is 'being Tobias', characteristically dispensing alcohol;

Edna starts to assume Agnes's role, 'becoming Agnes' and reproving Julia. This mirrors the newcomers' contention that they belong and are wanted. Albee merges the couples and blurs their identities.

As the second act concludes Agnes and Edna turn in parallel moments to Tobias, and the merging produces a question of choice

AGNES: . . . Tobias?
   (*Exits with* JULIA. *Silence.*)
EDNA: Well, *I* think it's time for bed.
TOBIAS (*vague, preoccupied*): Well, yes; yes, of course.
EDNA (*she and* HARRY *have risen; a small smile*): We know the way.
   (*Pauses as she and* HARRY *near the archway.*)
   Friendship *is* something like a marriage, is it not, Tobias? For better and for worse?
TOBIAS (*ibid.*): Sure.
EDNA (*something of a demand here*): We *haven't* come to the wrong place, *have* we?
HARRY (*pause; shy*): Have we, Toby?
TOBIAS (*pause; gentle, sad*): No.
   (*Sad smile.*) No; of course you haven't.

This transformation makes clear in theatrical terms the threat posed by the friends and by their fear. The society which Albee creates is at once both strange and familiar; recognisable and impossible. The claims of family and friendship are in conflict, and then blended together. Julia demands of Tobias that he throw out Harry and Edna as interlopers; in their transformation he confronts them as an integral part of the household. The merging of the couples creates a meld of the values of marriage and friendship as relationships to be suffered 'for better and for worse'. The vocabulary of a society built in such a way is a vocabulary of rights to be demanded. At crucial moments such rights are transformed into primitive violent demands. When the issue is ultimately put to Tobias, Albee has the means of suggesting other bases to his response than force of circumstances.

Throughout the play Tobias serves as the focus for the issues of choice and responsibility, his sad ineffectuality sensitising the audience to the moral and emotional values which are so severely compromised. Ultimately attention rests on the want of real values to sustain a choice, and on the moral weakness which attaches to Tobias as the father of the family. This absence is linked with Albee's characteristic breakdown of the family, and the loss of the child. When Julia returns, Agnes recalls the moment when the family broke apart. After the death of their son, notably seen as usurper by the child Julia, their love was no longer clear, or even possible.

> AGNES: Nothing is calmed by a pat on the hand, a gentle massage, or slowly combing the hair, no: the history. Teddy's birth and how she felt unwanted, tricked; his death, and was she more relieved than lost . . .? All the schools we sent her to, and did she fail in them through hate . . . or love?

The absent child is now a familiar theme, and here the treatment is yet closer to the dramatist's private mythology. The child who died is called Teddy, and Albee is too meticulous for the diminutive of his own name to be oversight. (This recalls O'Neill's use of his name for the dead child in *Long Day's Journey Into Night*.) Even the reference's to Julia's failures at school, and the enigmatic reference to the child's distorted cry for love are strikingly close to Albee's life. The loss of this love is the subject of the play, and it is experienced in the central role of Tobias and exposed in his crisis of choice.

The structuring of the role combines a series of weak responses to the demands of the action, combined with a strained attention to the undercurrents of the developing situation. The ineffectuality is not ineptitude, but moral weakness and repression. Technically the actor is given little on which to build save the repeated defence he mounts against the implied attacks, and rare moments of almost operatic expressiveness. These are all the more striking for their placing in a role which does not dominate the stage. When Tobias tells the story of the cat, like Jerry's similar parable of the dog, the actor is able to distill the crisis of emotion that the play investigates. Tobias felt love as a demand – a want – which led him to kill the creature when it refused to love him. The brutality of the story contradicts the mildness of the role elsewhere and explains the currents of strain which erupt in the final act.

The lost child is of course the narrative detail which completes the pattern. In *A Delicate Balance* Albee makes a particular use of the motif, exploring further the implications of loss and the painful intrusion of reality into the lives of his characters. The loss of Tobias's son is linked to the question of choice and the ultimate value of life. As the actor avoids the incursions of the other performers – all actresses as far as the process goes – the initial reaction to his son's death is each time re-created. Above all, the avoidance takes the form of a plea. At the beginning of Act III, after a wakeful night, Tobias is found early on Sunday morning by Agnes. We learn that the state of the house has meant that Tobias has, at least for an hour or two, shared a room with his wife, a thing he has not done for many years. Albee writes partly for the power and shock of the revelation, but also to characterise the moral pressure which Agnes exerts. She is aware of life but depends upon his choice:

> I am almost too old to be a grandmother as I'd hoped . . . too young to be one. Oh, I had wanted that: the *youngest* older woman on the block. *Julia* is almost too old to have a child properly; *will* be if she ever does . . . if she marries again. *You* could have pushed her back . . . if you'd wanted to.
>
> TOBIAS (*bewildered incredulity*): It's very early yet: that must be it. I've never heard such . . .
>
> AGNES: Or Teddy! No? No stammering here? You'll let this pass?
>
> TOBIAS (*quiet embarrassment*): Please.

The separation of the couple, which is felt subliminally throughout the play, is explicitly related to Tobias's refusal to face reality. The choices which the women expect of him are not hierarchical, as might be suspected in a family play of this sort. They are the choices which arise because of the interactions which are inevitable in life, and from which no one can withdraw. This is what Edna makes clear to Julia from the strange position she adopts in the house, and which is made impressively explicit when Agnes confronts Tobias. By avoidance Tobias has chosen uninvolvement and built a family on his fears. Albee directs the actress to put the facts in a 'remorseless' fashion:

> When Teddy died?
> (*Pause.*)
> We *could* have had another son; we could have tried. But no . . . those months – or was it a year – ?

TOBIAS: No more of this!

AGNES: . . . I think it was a year, when you spilled yourself on my belly, sir? 'Please? Please, Tobias?' No, you wouldn't even say it out: I don't want another child, another loss. 'Please? Please, Tobias?' And guiding you, *trying* to hold you in?

The frankness of the writing intensifies the pressure of the choice being imposed. Relationships are felt here to involve life and the risk of loss or damage. The climactic movement of the play gains impetus from the revelation of the hurt that lies behind Agnes's delicate balance. The pressure of the past builds the audience's understanding of the moral and emotional value of Tobias's choice of action in receiving his friends or rejecting them. In him can be seen the fear which in other terms has destroyed the tranquillity of Harry and Edna

The conflicting claims on the home produce a dramatic event of considerable range, as the relationships within the family are exploited to mirror the dilemma of a society which lacks the means to build a true community. The family itself is not made a scapegoat and is not the source of the breakdown the play represents. The family is what society will allow. If the family is impoverished in this play, it is because Albee is exploring the barrenness of a community built on a false awareness of rights. In this play the right to belong is a demand, in the way that there is a primitive demand for affection. What is lost is the ability to give affection, to create a community out of love. At the moment Tobias makes his choice and allows his friends to stay, Albee writes an *aria*. He attempts to invest this set piece with a pressure of feeling which makes its meanings as amply as the ideas which are contained. It is a full-blown emotional act, releasing the pent-up tensions of the role

(*Soft*) You've put nearly forty years in it, baby; so have I, and if it's nothing, I don't give a damn, you've got the right to be here, you've earned it.

(*Loud*) AND BY GOD YOU'RE GOING TO TAKE IT!

DO YOU HEAR ME?

YOU BRING YOUR TERROR AND YOU COME IN HERE

AND YOU LIVE WITH US!

YOU BRING YOUR PLAGUE!

YOU STAY WITH US!

I DON'T WANT YOU HERE!

I DON'T LOVE YOU!

BUT BY GOD . . . YOU STAY!!

The stage direction requires 'all the horror and exuberance of a man who has kept his emotions under control for too long'. The horror comes from recognition, but the exuberance from action. There is no simple idealism in all this and certainly no Albee message. Tobias faces up to the lack of love and the substitution of almost propietarial rights; and the most that he can do is to act and confront the problem, accepting their right to stay. Tobias's tearful plea to his friends to stay expresses no affection, only a decision to recognise the need to build a community.

Inevitably Harry and Edna quietly leave, with Edna modulating the ideas of Tobias's aria in her acceptance that they too have looked back over a life and 'still have not learned . . . the boundaries, what we may not do . . . not ask, for fear of looking in a mirror'. The fear is the fear of confrontation: in the mirror or in one's neighbour one sees oneself. The energy of the play survives the recognition of the risk of a community and the choice of action, but it shows a parting of the ways. Harry and Edna leave with the promise that they will not 'be strangers', Julia may perhaps go back to her husband – she is fond of marriage, as she wittily remarks; and Agnes reminds them all of the temptation of madness. There is, despite the danger of breakdown, at least a residue of energy, and the vaguest sense of direction. More astonishing to Agnes than her belief that she will lose the balance of her mind is now 'the wonder of daylight, of the sun'. The balance is maintained with the acceptance of community.

6
'All Over'

In 1967 Albee announced that he was working on two short plays, 'Life' and 'Death', and that the first was developing into a long play. In the event both developed into full-length pieces, and it was 'Death' which was the first to be performed, in the version we now know as *All Over*, in March 1971 on Broadway. 'Life' was to come later: as *Seascape*, performed in 1975. Despite the fact that the plays exist as separate entities and came to performance years apart, they bear close comparison. The techniques of both show the lessons learned from the experiments of *Box* and *Quotations from Chairman Mao*. The dialogue resembles musical structure, particularly in *Seascape*, where the handling of the four parts has struck many critics as being 'string quartetish'. (Albee was seen in a BBC documentary study shortly afterwards listening to Mozart quartets and looking out onto the seascape at his Montauk country home.) *All Over* was more aply qualified as having the character of an oratorio, given its greater dependence on virtual monologue, and other extended speeches.

The pairing of these two works is most informative in the

contrasted perspectives which they adopt on life. Both present family life, and the succession of the human generations. For the couple Nancy and Charlie in *Seascape*, the family is a pyramid, building up beneath them; in *All Over* the family is rubble, the ruin of something that might have been. *Seascape* is unusual among Albee's works, adopting as it does an essentially optimistic outlook, in which the wit of the writing emerges delightfully. *All Over* is a bitter and melancholy play by turns. Although the terms may be unreliable in a modern context, it can seem that Albee set out originally to write a connected comedy and tragedy. There is no doubt that the plays share a fundamental similarity in the basic subject, realising the potential of an idea in contrasted moods. The image of the Mistress in *All Over* taking solitary walks along a beach in winter makes a pendant with the sunbathed beach of the couple in *Seascape*.

All Over has been accused of the mannerism which, for some critics, is the mark of Albee's exhaustion as an artist. The control of the style created difficulties with his Broadway audience, still waiting for a return to the freedom of the early plays. The characters are even more evidently articulate than in *A Delicate Balance*, and the parts are so written as to require a considerable measure of control in the performer, as well as sensitivity and intelligence in the rendering of some penetratingly observed behaviour. The play, as the dramatist felt obliged to point out, is a deeply felt piece of work. If the two plays – 'Life' and 'Death' – were to be connected, it was in their complementary treatment of the sense of value and purpose in life and the consequences which follow from what these are deemed to be. *All Over* treats the subject at the moment of dying, as opposed to the moment of death: a distinction which first appears in *Quotations from*

Chairman Mao and which is crucial here. One cannot *be* dead, but can have died, so the argument runs. And it is one which links the Long-Winded Lady in *Quotations from Chairman Mao* with the Mistress in *All Over*, as each attempts to come to terms with the loss of a partner. The value of life, it is implied, is not in being but in doing. Death is the conclusion of life, therefore in a sense an active process. When one is dead one is not.

The scene of *All Over* is the room of a celebrated and remarkable man who is now dying, attended by his Doctor and Nurse, and a family group: Wife, Son, Daughter, Best Friend and Mistress, who have assembled for what is described as a 'ritual': the deathwatch. (Albee's Playwrights Unit produced Genet's play in *Deathwatch* in the sixties. It uses a similar ritual of waiting and crisis, although here the resemblance ends.) The dying man, screened up-stage in a canopied four-poster, has played various roles in the lives of the waiting characters. For the Son and the Daughter he is the source of the love of which they have been deprived, and which stirs momentarily or is distorted into hatred or bitterness. To the Wife he is the love she knew briefly as a young wife but which she lost as she failed to grow into adulthood beside her husband. The Best friend mirrors this wasted marriage in his own divorce and in his guilt for his own wife's alienation and madness; and he looks back on a brief sad affair with the dying man's wife. To one side of the family is the figure of the Mistress, who won a different relationship by her willingness to accept love from a man whom she inevitably could not know. For her his death means the extinction of that love; for the others it is the occasion for a bleak assessment of their lives.

The events are observed by the Doctor and the Nurse, who fit easily and familiarly into the scene, being no strangers to death, 'the oldest disease', and who owe their ease to their activity: ministering to death makes it for them a significant but integral part of the process of life. While the deathwatch is maintained, outside are the public and the press, for the dying man was a figure of weight and importance beyond the circle of the family in the life of the nation.

Taken as a portrayal of a family in the process of disintegration, *All Over* can appear grotesque, a combination of unappetising characters and behaviour. Compared to *Seascape* it contains a suspicion of emotional hysteria which has been found to inhabit Albee's work from Jerry's self-immolation onwards. But plays are rarely realistic portrayals, and certainly not those of Albee. He has a neat dictum which may serve to describe *All Over*: 'A play is a fiction, and fiction is fact distorted into truth.' We are not affected by the bare 'facts' but by the 'distortions': in the way they are controlled and arranged for performance. In this respect Albee's control is manifest in *All Over*. In the Broadway production the abstract quality of the work was emphasised by isolating the realistic box set in the larger space of the stage, with the stage equipment visible all round: a small section of contrived 'reality' placed before an audience. In the same way the fragments of human behaviour Albee imagines are detached from life via the process which the dramatist likes to call composition. The coolness of the method is in stark contrast to some of the material he uses. The Daughter, for example, lives with a man who beats her and steals her money. He in turn has an alcoholic wife whom he abuses and supplies with liquor. In addition he has involved the family in the suppression of a scandal involving him with the Mafia. Albee uses these scraps to furnish the debris of lives which have been lived with varying degrees of waste, and never interests us in the life stories. He needs only a few sharp thrusts as the characters engage, and the weapons he imagines must be capable of inflicting damage.

All Over inevitably centres on the classic antagonists – Wife and Mistress; but in various ways Albee makes the rivals allies and the axis of his play. The roles are linked through the common experience of this death and its shared significance. The superficial interpretation is given to the Daughter:

> This woman has come and taken . . . my . . . father!
> THE WIFE (*after a pause; not sad; a little weary; empty, perhaps*): Yes. My *hus*band. Remember?
> This woman loves my husband – as *I* do – and she has made him happy; as I have. She is good, and decent, and she is not moved by envy and self-loathing.

It is the children who are set in opposition to the Wife. This is not to say that, in Harold Hobson's phrase, the play is 'a melancholy judgement . . . on the institution of the family'. It is at times a melancholy spectacle; but it is not a play about family life. It is about life. The accent is upon the backward look and the reassessment of how a life has been lived. The children are casualties, for this has not been done honestly, and it is notable that Albee does not feel the need to spell out all the reasons. One critic, Stenz, assuming the need for a naturalistic character background, is led to surmise what has warped the children:

> the kinds of unrealistic standards the parents upheld for them to imitate and the kinds of restrictions they imposed contributed to what resulted in one case in behaviour that took the form of an extreme reaction and in the other in the destruction of all initiative.[34]

This answer would be helpful if the play ever posed the question, but it does not. This is a pointer to the way it works. Albee does not offer explanations or justifications: they would suggest easy answers.

The Mistress tells a story of the quarrels of two other children. Like the children of the play they were stunted: 'two elderly children who didn't like each other very much'. Perhaps the reason was that the daughter had married unwisely for a second time, but really the reasons are unimportant: 'the reasons went further back, the dislike for some genesis I came upon them too late for . . . The cause comes not to matter. Only the capacity for damage in the present.' Albee's method highlights the individual's capacity, not the explanation of his weaknesses. Of course the past determines the present, but the play concentrates upon failure in the past as the misuse of capacity, damage done as well as suffered. It is the chain of actions which counts. On occasions this is violently demonstrated in the play. When the Wife pleasantly tells the Mistress of a time when her husband inquired if these were indeed his children, the Daughter walks across to her 'almost languidly' and slaps her across the face. Albee writes an identical stage direction for the seventy-year-old woman to return the blow. This shows well the combination of rage and distortion which exists within the relationship, as well as the unnerving indifference: the lack of 'evident emotion' which is demonstrated. What we see is violence with a strange lack of engagement between the characters. The method is essentially dramatic, giving us events, not explanations. The reactions to these events will be complex, depending on the spectator's sensitivity to the failure which is built into the interactions at some point. The Son's grieving at a remove, over his father's bathroom and personal possessions, is the image of his remoteness and his immaturity. Albee brings out the pattern of destruction in the response of his mother, who unfeelingly treats him as the whining child he effectively is: 'Give us you, and you find a BATHROOM MOVING?'

The brutality of the attacks demands a response from the audience, and inevitably a desire to understand and apportion blame for the damage which they see inflicted. Albee gives direction to this, but not by supplying missing links. Instead he exposes the pity of not having lived a life and the weakness which is the inevitable result. The Wife's attacks on the Son are at one point witnessed by the Daughter, who sits in the classical attitude of grief, with her arm thrown across her face. It is a rare moment of compassion in the part:

> He's spent his grown life getting set against everything, fobbing it all off, covering his shit as best he can, and so what if the sight of one unexpected ludicrous thing collapses it all? So *what*! It's proof, isn't it? Isn't it proof he's not as . . . little as you said he was? It is you know.
> (*Slight pause.*)
> You make me as sick as I make you.

The children fight, or defend themselves as best they can. The spectacle is alternatively ugly and pathetic. Their disaster is that they have nothing to defend. With the death of the father it is clear that there is nothing for any of them. The Wife's contempt is directed at them, but it is the family as a whole which has failed.

> You've neither of you had children, thank God, children that I've known of.
> (*Harsh*) I hope you never marry . . . *either* of you!
> (*Softer, if no gentler*) Let the line end where it is . . . at its zenith.

All Over

Albee deepens the audience's experience of this failure by counterpointing the skirmishes with long speeches functioning almost like musical movements, and in which he can shift the audience's attention away from the particular interactions of his cast and towards related expressions of his themes. He avoids specific reference to responsibility in the family, and widens the perspective on life. It also allows considerable alterations in mood and therefore in audience experience.

One such speech conveys the failure of a life in the image of premature death. The Wife recalls her aunt who, for unspecified reasons, 'died in the heart' at the age of twenty-six, but who lived on until she was 'snuffed out' in a car accident, 'her twenty-six-year heart emptying out her sixty-two-year body'. The particular scene the Wife recalls makes an important impression for the play as a whole

> 'Does anyone love me?' she asked once, back when I was nine or ten. There were several of us in the room, but they were used to it. 'Do you love anyone?' I asked her back. Slap! Then tears – hers and mine; mine not from the pain but the . . . effrontery; hers . . . both; effrontery and pain.

The story is prompted by the dialogue which precedes: the Daughter demanding fiercely if she is loved by *anyone*, and the Wife, suddenly becoming serious, turning the question back on her. The demand is used as a motif in a way characteristic of the composition as a whole. It is a fierce, animal act and is placed periodically through the action in the roles of both the Daughter and the Wife. The Mistress articulates at a late stage in the play how the Daughter has only animal ferocity with which to defend herself, and, if ever she comes to know love, she will have no words to translate her joy. All she will have will be 'the snarl of a wounded and wounding animal'. Thus Albee directs the actress to play the Daughter's demand for her mother's attention in Act II as 'a growl' and then 'a howl'. The Wife's action is less of a demand than a defence, for she has long since lost the love of the dying man. However, in her ending of the two acts her need is again expressed in animal ferocity. When the press are brought into the room at the conclusion of Act I she screams at them with 'a beast's voice' and 'finally; it is an animal's sound'. At the end of Act II her cry is different: more complex and expressive of her recognition of 'all that has been pent up for thirty years'.

This violent physical performance communicates a need which is readily felt throughout the play. It is also contrasted with the articulated style in which Albee refines the physical experience into a more distinct moral view. The impact of the play can be seen in the highly musical scoring of the physical effort of the Wife's final lines, but also in the ideas of her ultimate rejection of the family she helped create:

> All we've done . . . is think of ourselves.
> (*Pause.*)
> Selfless love? *I* don't think so; we love to *be* loved, and when it's taken away . . . then why *not* rage . . . pule.
> (*Pause.*)
> All we've *done* is think about ourselves. Ultimately.

The counterbalance to this waste and ruin appears in the minor figures of the Doctor and the Nurse and is richly developed in the Mistress. Both the Doctor and the Nurse are at ease with death, and somehow immune to its threat. The Mistress admires the eighty-year-old physician's survival 'in the midst of the contagions' and he replies that, like the priest in the old days of the plague, he has a function which safeguards him. Why does he not retire? He has not slept, he says, for forty years. The answer is that he has things to *do*, in contrast to those who do nothing but think of themselves. Both the Doctor and the Nurse are given narrations in which the ideas of the play are developed with a particular mood and accent.

The Doctor has a tale of doing service in the prisons: his 'tithe'. He recalls how the condemned prisoners sometimes 'made love to themselves in a frenzy' and, with a distinct overtone of Genet, Albee identifies the prisoners' masturbatory image with the executioner. The Doctor explains the point of his story as reflecting his own identification of love and death. He feels warm physical affection for the grandson who candidly and naturally announces to him that he must soon die. Love and death are not at odds.

His recollections expose a contrast in the play between those who withdraw in the face of death and those for whom it reinforces life and love. The Nurse with her one narrative adds a dimension to the contrast. She has a robust attitude to life and death, out of tune with the defeatism of the Son. She calmly announces that he is too fat and will not last past his fifties:

> two whiskies before dinner, a glass of good burgundy
> *with* it, and sex before you go to sleep. That'll do the
> trick, keep you going.
>
> THE SON: For?
>
> THE NURSE (*rather surprised at the question*): Until it is
> time for you to die. No point in rushing it.

She has the sort of hearty commitment to life which the Son is inacapable of giving. The Nurse's story arises out of her love, a fact which surprises the Wife. She was mistress of the last family doctor and tells how the story had been given out that he died on the *Titanic*, when in fact he went quietly to his fishing-lodge in Maine and shot himself: 'I mean, if the cancer's on you and you're a doctor to boot and you know the chances *and* the pain, well . . . what do you do save book on a boat you think is going to run into an iceberg and sink.' The joke about the *Titanic* suggests the heroic scale of the doctor's recognition of death, and in the text it replies to the Wife's remembrance of a time when she shared life with her husband; when he had not 'closed down' and 'the titans were still engaged'.

Life has a heroic dimension to it, and this is brought home in attitudes to death. In exploring the attitudes of his characters, Albee invests each with a distinct moral value. This explains the most important relationship in the play: the contrast between the Wife and the Mistress. The opening dialogue gives the germ of their alternative views on life. The Wife's question 'Is he dead?' brings an objection from the Mistress, who remembers her lover's insistence that 'one could be dying or have died . . . but could not . . . be . . . dead'. She recognises the value of being, and its obligations. This is understood by the Wife only in the closing moments of the play The Mistress reflects on the Doctor's practice with 'some wonder' as 'sixty years of something'. When the Wife discovers that the Nurse has been a man's mistress she is amazed, having not considered the woman as a person at all, but rather 'a presence'. The two women are aware in different ways of the quality which makes a life. The Mistress warmly admires 'something'; the Wife is naïvely struck by the realisation that the Nurse is a 'presence'. The terms are abstract but embody critical meanings in the play. They also supply a vocabulary for the discussion of the two women's lives. The Wife has a significant refrain: as she waits out her marriage she thinks 'the little girl I was when he came to me'. From time to time she repeats this 'like the announcement of a subject'. Later the Mistress muses, comparing the two of them, 'I wonder: if I had been *you* – the little girl you were when he came to you – would you have come along, as I did. Would you have come to take my place?' This comparison is enlarged by the play, for the women differ in more respects than the accident of which knew the dying man first.

The comparison is engineered in a variety of ways: even when the Mistress confronts the Daughter, her remarks are assumed by the Wife:

THE MISTRESS: You are not a very kind woman.

THE WIFE: She has been raised at her mother's knee.

The wasteful relationship of mother and daughter is rooted in the immaturity they both exhibit. Notably the Mistress applies to the Daughter the same term, 'little girl'. When the Mistress calls the Daughter an amateur in love, she describes a love which the Wife conspicuously lacks: 'Love with mercy, I mean, the kind that you can't hold back as a reward, or use as any sort of weapon.' This well describes the way the family has destroyed itself, and the Wife is similarly an amateur despite the years in which she was still in contact with her husband. The story of her young love and marriage, which comes at the end of the play, is quite different from that of the Mistress's summer affair. It was the love of 'a little girl', 'no summer lovemaking; no thought to it, or anything like it; alas'. Her husband made her feel twelve years old.

> I had never felt threatened, by boys, but he was a man and I felt secure.

THE MISTRESS: Did you fall in love at once?
THE WIFE: Hmm? (*Thinks about it.*)

I don't *know*: I knew that I would marry him, that he would ask me, and it seemed very . . . right. I felt calm. Is that an emotion? I suppose it is.

Hard on the heels of this speculation comes the Wife's realisation that no one has mattered since those days. The stage direction is 'with loss': 'I don't love *you*. (*The* MISTRESS *nods, looks away*.) I don't love *anyone*.' And when she affirms her love for her husband it is still a version of the animal demand, 'an enraged shout which has her quivering'. In this role emotions have not grown beyond the infantile. The moment in which she recognises her thirty years of waste follows, and it is a combination of the animal need and the beginnings of honest engagement with life. Albee gives careful stage directions to get the vocal quality he needs, and to explain the significance of the breakdown 'It explodes from her, finally, all that has been pent up for thirty years. It is loud, broken by sobs and gulps of air; it is self-pitying and self-loathing; pain and relief.'

In these final speeches Albee produces his chosen form of resolution, which reflects the technique of classical tragedy: recognition, reversal and an emotional catharsis. The significance of the Wife and of her relationship to the Son and Daughter is felt in the physical flow of the breakdown. In the face of the loss of love, the Wife says, why not 'rage . . . or pule'. These are the reactions of her daughter and her son and she herself combines them in the pent-up self-loathing and self-pity of the lost years, embittered emotions which she has nurtured in her own home.

The Mistress is a sensitive reflection, at every stage, of the failures of the family group. She herself remembers that the things she received from the dying man were company, love and a sense of values; the Wife received only the security of a little girl. Albee uses his extended speeches to give a warm theatrical expression of the values he intends. Thus the Mistress has a series of set speeches which reflect a contrasting attitude to life. Describing her lover at Christmas time, she explains the need to give:

> I caught his profile as he stared into the fire, that . . . marvellous granite, and it was as if he had . . . deflated, just perceptibly. I took his hand, and he turned to me and smiled: came back. I said, 'You should spend it with *them*; every *year*.'

The speeches are meticulously written to allow the point both to be made and to be emotionally re-created, completing the experience of compassion and generosity for the audience. When the actress later has speeches describing the Mistress's parents, the stage directions make clear Albee's intention of creating experience: 'some delight; really to bring them all back'. Her amused description of the old couple venturing forth in a car is greeted with incomprehension by her listeners. Albee uses the exchanges to make clear a scale of values:

> THE BEST FRIEND: Why doesn't *she* drive?
> THE MISTRESS (*smiles a little*): No; she could learn, but I imagine she'd rather sit there and see things his way.
> THE DAUGHTER (*dry*): Why doesn't she walk, or take a taxi, or just not go?
> THE MISTRESS (*knows she is being mocked, but prefers to teach rather than hit back*): Oh; she loves him, you see.

The Mistress has known love and selflessness in her parents. She has in her own life demanded nothing from

111

her lover, nor did she ever wish to possess either of the men whom she married and from whom she was separated only by death. Side by side with the Wife's dispassionate account of her courtship and marriage, Albee writes the Mistress's account of her first love. It contains more than a hint of Tennessee Williams's *Sweet Bird of Youth*.

That was back, very far, fifteen and sixteen. God! we were in love: innocent, virgins, both of us, and I doubt that either of us had ever told a lie. We met by chance at a lawn party on a Sunday afternoon, and had got ourselves in bed by dusk. You may not call that love, but it was. We were not embarrassed children, awkward and puppy-rutting. No; fifteen and sixteen, and never been before, but our sex was a strong and practiced and assisting . . . 'known' thing between us, from the very start . . .

We were a man and a woman . . . an uncorrupted man and woman, and we made love all the summer, every day, wherever, whenever.

For an example of corruption the audience has the other summer affair of the Wife and the Best Friend. That is described with mild disgust and associated with the collapse of the Best Friend's marriage. Albee maps out in this way a composition of ideas and attitudes which exposes the degree of commitment and generosity in each of the roles. Ultimately he achieves a tension in his audience between two sorts of feeling and two ideas of the significance of loss, his perennial theme. The play is plainly concerned with parting, and the assessment of past time: every character is given his or her moment to reflect this. The Mistress and the Wife both register a deeply expressive loss, but the retrospective which Albee employs makes its moral quality quite distinct. If life has been lived well, there is the loss of something which might go on; if badly, there is only the bitter experience of waste. The Mistress has a poignant speech in which she imagines what she will do in the future:

> I think what I shall do is go to where I've been, *we've* been, but I shall do it out of focus, for indeed it will be. I'll go to Deauville in October, with only the Normandie open, and take long wrapped-up walks along the beach in the cold and gray. I'll spend a week in Copenhagen when the Tivoli's closed. And I'll have my Christmas in Venice, where I'm told it usually snows. Or maybe I'll go to Berlin and stare at the wall. We were there when they put it up. There's so much one can do. And so little.

There is a yearning quality of life in this writing which is contrasted with the Wife's dull desire for something that she can *feel*. With his taste for gentle allegory Albee attaches wider meanings to the inner rottenness of this imagined dynasty. There is little detail of the public life of his characters. We need nothing more than the few allusions to the power and influence of the dying man, giving the sense of the outside world with its illusions of the life of the great. This supplies the tension Albee requires. The implications of the values which he dissects in *All Over* are felt in the wider political sphere, hence the reference to the Berlin Wall, which specifies the denial of life in the relations between peoples. Albee is moved by his sense of the value of a society to compose plays which operate in terms of the nuclear relationships of men, women and families, but in which a complex moral pattern emerges. The approach in *All Over* shows an increasing confidence in handling the pattern, while preserving the dramatist's theatrical taste for tension and strong effects. The latent violence of his plays is here undiminished, but the spectacular moments are more tightly focused by the expression of the emotional forces and the moral possibilities which are in play. His writing remains agreeably shocking, but increases still further the depth of inquiry required of the audience

The demand on the audience met with a poor response in New York, where the play ran for only forty-four performances. On the other hand, the London production by the Royal Shakespeare Company was highly successful, and was been particularly admired by the playwright himself. Similarly, the play was well received internationally. The explanation is hardly to do with the sour view of society which is part of Albee's vision. Albee at his most evidently un-American (which he is not) in *The American Dream* was Albee at the height of his popularity. More likely is the difficulty produced by the development of Albee's art in the late sixties and his progressive use of a more abstract style. As he had made clear, Broadway does not supply the context for the reception of serious drama, even when, as for *All Over* there is some warmth in the reception of the critical press. The context in which Albee can locate his plays as a writer is undoubtedly European, although the inspiration remains undeniably American. It is ironical that, in a play which sees Albee refining his techniques and producing a composition of great depth and expressiveness, he should not find on Broadway an audience with an equal depth of recognition. His next play, *Seascape*, was to be carefully prepared for Broadway with a two-month tour. And it was to be directed by Albee.

7
'Seascape'

Long before the first performance of *Seascape* Albee
teased his questioners over what it would contain. 'I'm
moving from writing about people to writing about
animals', he declared, and later described the play as a 'true
to life story'. His audience could hardly have been
prepared for the play they attended in January 1975. Many
of the Albee ingredients are there. There is the married
couple face to face with the problems of what is reality in
their lives, and there is the intrusion of a second couple to
create the quartet for which he writes so fluently.

When the setting is a holiday beach, and the atmosphere
is one of love and seductive contentment, the scene
seems strangely anodyne; but, when the crisis is provoked
by two giant humanoid lizards crawling up from the
primeval depths of the sea, then the result is something
quite new. When he says that he is writing about animals
Albee is teasing, but at the same time that is precisely what
he is doing. Commentators who obstinately concentrate on
the familial struggles in his plays ignore the fact that he

115

writes in a wider context: a society, a way of life, even a species. *Seascape* is an important development in this process in that it treats the question of the future of the species.

It appears in the opening seconds of the play in a purely theatrical image that includes the seeds of much of what follows:

> *The curtain rises.* NANCY *and* CHARLIE *on a sand dune. Bright sun. They are dressed informally. There is a blanket and a picnic basket. Lunch is done;* NANCY *is finishing putting things away. There is a pause and then a jet plane is heard from stage right to stage left – growing, becoming deafeningly loud, diminishing.*

NANCY: Such noise they make.

CHARLIE: They'll crash into the dunes one day. I don't know what good they do.

NANCY (*looks toward the ocean; sighs*): Still . . . Oh, Charlie, it's so nice! Can't we stay here forever? Please!

There is the hint of apocalypse in Charlie's resentment of the noise and a yearning for a truer life in Nancy's delighted fascination with the seascape. (The same sort of combination of images is found in Elizabeth's dream of the holocaust in the final moments of *The Lady from Dubuque*.) From time to time the sound of the 'plane returns to overshadow the events of the play, as they bring into perspective a view of life which Albee has not developed elsewhere on such a scale. There are suggestions of the dimensions to life as early as *The Zoo Story*, when Jerry explains that, to break out of isolation, *some* contact must be found:

it's just that if you can't deal with people, you have to make a start somewhere, WITH ANIMALS.

(*Much faster now and like a conspirator*) Don't you see? A person has to have some way of dealing with SOMETHING . . .

In *Seascape* Albee escapes the particular social contexts within which he normally writes in order to consider in a fundamental way the phenomenon we know as life and experience personally as existence.

The action of *Seascape* is elegantly simple. Nancy and Charlie are a warm, affectionate couple now entering their retirement. As they picnic by the seaside Nancy enthuses about the natural life around, and, wishing it were possible, innocently suggests that they should live always like this. Beside the sea. Always moving on in the sun.

> One great seashore after another; the pounding waves and quiet coves; white sand, and red and black, somewhere, I remember reading; palms, and pine trees, cliffs and reefs, and miles of jungle, sand dunes
> . . .
> CHARLIE: No.
> NANCY: . . . and all the people! Every language . . . every
> . . . race.

Charlie's refusal to consider Nancy's eccentric fancies is a contrast to the recollection she elicits from him that when he was a child he loved to escape down into the sea. Unlike his friends, who dreamed (significantly) of flight, he imagined himself 'a regular fish . . . fishlike arms and legs and everything, but able to go under'. As the couple reflect on their past life, including its moments of tension, a picture emerges of their fidelity and warm interdependence. The conflict appears now at the point where the children are grown – 'nicely settled . . . to all appearances' – and the next generation has begun. Having done what they 'ought to do', they are at the point where they have new choices. As Nancy puts it, 'now we've got each other and some time, and all *you* want to do is become a vegetable'.

With the appearance of the two talking reptiles Sarah and Leslie, there is a more urgent confrontation. There is the threat of violence as the males face one another, but this gives way to the struggle they experience in explaining and, inevitably, evaluating what their lives are like. The climax of the play is produced as Charlie tries to explain how the four of them are part of a process of evolution. As he and Nancy attempt to explain the concept to their new friends, the images of life on land and in the sea are drawn together, and the truth emerges that what they are all involved in together is the progess of life. Charlie is moved, much to Nancy's wonder, from his inertia of the opening of the play to a demand that Sarah and Leslie accept emotion – which is expressed in the play as a feeling for the life in you. As the quartet weathers the storm of this new emotion, the sea creatures are persuaded to stay and adapt to the new life they have encountered and help the unfamiliar creatures they recognise as their fellows.

Very often there is a distinct reminiscence of *All Over*, suggesting an alternative presentation of similar material. In *All Over* the family appeared synonymous with sterility and failure. This is reversed in *Seascape*. Nancy plays with the engaging image of the pyramid of succeeding generations. They have succeeded but she knows the risks:

> everybody builds his own, starts fresh, starts up in the air, builds the base around him. Such levitation! Our own have started *theirs*! . . .

. . . Or maybe it's the most . . . difficult, the most . . . breathtaking of all: the whole thing balanced on one point; a reversed *pyramid*, always in danger of toppling over when people don't behave themselves.

Nancy has lived her life looking forward. From the earliest days she wanted to be a woman: she wanted to grow up, unlike the Wife, who felt twelve years old when her husband came to her. There are two different values to the security the women see in their husbands: in *All Over* it is a security which involves an abdication in the face of life: in *Seascape* it is a progressive building, aware of the dangers but full of love and compassion.

The dangers are visible in the story of Charlie's seven months of depression, an episode which Albee invests with a particular richness of expression. At the heart of it is the idea of life as involving choice. The narration includes the choices that might have been: *if* Charlie had been unfaithful, *if* she had known other lovers; the consequences are worked out in the speech. Despite the fact that it all *was not*, Nancy learned and grew. 'The deeper your inertia went, the more *I* felt alive', says Nancy, and over the span of the narration the feeling for life is translated into the understanding present in a mature, even weatherbeaten, relationship. She recalls her mother's advice ('wise woman') and the stages of compassion: experiencing her own loneliness, and understanding *his*.

The picture is very much that of the Mistress in *All Over* and her compassion for her lover in, for instance, his loneliness on being separated from his family. Even the precision of language in the two characters is similar. Like the Mistress, Nancy insists on the importance of the tense of a verb: 'Am not *having*? Am not *having* a good life? . . . I know the language, and I know *you*. You're not careless with it, or didn't used to be.'

In *Seascape* Albee writes with energy about the potential there is in life, which largely he invests in the role of Nancy. Against this comes intermittent resistance in the character of Charlie. In much of the action of the first act there is a contest between Charlie's theme – 'Well, we've earned a little rest' – and Nancy's determination to avoid the 'purgatory before the purgatory': 'I haven't come this long way . . . Nor have you! Not this long way to let loose. All the wisdom – by accident, some of it – all the wisdom and the . . . unfettering.'

Albee finds the everyday phrase and exploits its deeper meaning. Charlie is 'happy . . . doing . . . nothing'. He spells out his conviction and the dramatist anatomises it in a 'testy' exchange between the two. As Nancy 'busily' tidies up and Charlie refuses to move, she challenges the absurdity of giving up on life:

> We are not going to be around forever, Charlie, and you may *not* do nothing. If you don't want to do what I want to do – which doesn't matter – then we will do what *you* want to do, but we will not do nothing. We will do something.

There is a delightful comedy to this combination of the philosophical and the domestic, and it sets the tone for the play as a whole. In all his work Albee shows a fine intelligence, and the comic viewpoint is rarely far off. It is, however, rare to find the humour that there is in *Seascape*: a fundamentally positive sense of life which, together with the compassion Albee always exhibits, makes *Seascape* an exceptional piece of work.

The comedy gathers momentum with the appearance of

the sea creatures and so too does the density of thought which is worked into the play. Albee manages a sustained flow of questions about social and individual existence through the agency of his monsters. Initially Charlie refuses to believe what his eyes tell him. The answer to these 'wonders' – and in his direction of the original production Albee required that they really be quite frightening – is characteristically to choose to believe in death:

> We ate the liver paste and we died. That drowsy feeling . . . the sun . . . and the wine . . . none of it: all those night thoughts of what it would be like, the sudden scalding in the centre of the chest, or wasting away; milk in the eyes, voices from the other room; none of it. Chew your warm sandwich, wash it down, lie back, and let the poison have its way . . .

Nancy's reaction is to instruct Charlie to roll over like an animal and adopt a submission pose. Natural enough in the meeting of two sort of animals. Albee bridges his acts with this image of the lizards and the submitting humans, and it is a delightful piece of theatrical fun. Especially when the newcomers, who are reflections of the first couple, open the second act with a somewhat disdainful discussion of the panic they have provoked: 'Well . . . they don't look very formidable – in the sense of prepossessing. Not young. They've got their teeth bared, but they don't look as if they are going to bite. Their hide is funny – feels soft.'

What follows is a true comedy of manners. Charlie and Nancy have to negotiate every step of the way their exchanges with these imagined representatives of another line of evolution.

SARAH: This is Leslie.

NANCY (*extending her hand*): How do you do, Leslie?

LESLIE (*regards her gesture*): What is that?

NANCY: Oh; we . . . well, we shake hands . . . flippers, uh
   . . . Charlie?

Sarah is delighted to learn of the gesture, whereas Leslie, who adopts Charlie's brand of negative rationalism, is unconvinced and wishes to know why it is done. When Charlie, progressively more involved, explains the significance of the proffered right hand, Leslie is equally defensive in his manner:

> it used to be to prove nobody had a weapon, to prove they were friendly.

LESLIE (*after a bit*): We're ambidextrous.

CHARLIE (*rather miffed*): Well, that's *nice* for you. Very nice.

The essence of the comedy lies in the wonder that each couple presents for the other, and in the parallelism that Albee devises to show up inflexibility, particularly of the males' position. In the females there is a parallel sense of wonder but an eager curiosity about what the new encounter may contain. Clothing and 'decency', for example, are concepts the scaly newcomers require to be defined, and Albee's idea drives a neat wedge between the human couple. The effect is to make comedy out of social manners but also to suggest the gradual awakening of Charlie from his somnolent attitudes to his wife and his life in general. Nancy teaches by the direct method and invites Sarah to see her breasts. To Charlie's great dismay Sarah, full of wonder and excitement, calls her mate Leslie to see. When Charlie objects, Leslie adopts a suitable nonchalance:

It's up to *you*; I mean, if they're something you *hide*, then may be they're embarrassing, or sad, and I shouldn't *want* to see them, and . . .

CHARLIE (*more flustered than angry*): They're not embarrassing; or *sad*; They're lovely! Some women . . . some women Nancy's age, they're . . . some women . . .

(*To* NANCY, *almost spontaneously bursting into tears*) I *love* your breasts.

With great skill Albee contrives a debate to combine the sharply differentiated reactions and characteristics in the four roles and a shifting discussion of various aspects of the new experience that the characters are called on to live. The subjects include marriage customs, flight and aerodynamics, child-bearing and rearing, and racialism. Albee establishes some hold over the form of the act by centring the conflicts in Charlie's progressive involvement. He makes one retreat into the negative rationalism he shares with Leslie when he staunchly reaffirms in the face of the facts that they are dead. Nancy explains

I mean, we *have* to be dead, because Charlie has decided that the wonders do not occur; that what we have not known does not exist; that what we cannot fathom cannot be; that the miracles, if you will, are bedtime stories; he has taken the leap of faith, from agnostic to atheist; the world is flat; the sun and the planets revolve around it, and don't row out too far or you'll fall off.

This prompts a most elegantly ridiculous routine as Leslie the lizard engages Charlie in a discussion of the nature of existence and the theories of Descartes

LESLIE: Then I take it *we* don't *exist*.

CHARLIE (*apologetic*): Probably not; I'm sorry.

LESLIE (*to* NANCY): That's quite a mind he's got there. (. . .)

LESLIE (*to* CHARLIE): You mean it's all an illusion?

CHARLIE: Could be.

LESLIE: The whole thing? Existence?

CHARLIE: Um-hum!

LESLIE (*sitting down with* CHARLIE): I don't believe *that* at all.

Like meets like in the encounter and Leslie's dogged pursuit of the discussions runs into Charlie's hysterical rage as he has to explain Descartes's *Cogito*.

Charlie is reassured of the physical fact of his existence by a particularly lengthy and passionate embrace from Nancy, and this, together with the lizards' panic at another passing jet, brings him finally face to face with the 'wonders'. Albee gives the stage direction 'Awe' at this point.

The creatures can be seen as a threat but they are an aspect of the wonder of life. They are animals with whom Charlie shares life and with whom he can make a society. Albee consolidates the shift in the role with Nancy's proud revelation to her new companions that there was a time when Charlie escaped from the world 'up here' by diving down to the bottom of the sea – unlike his fellows who wished to take to the air and, implicitly, join the noise of the jets. Charlie is uneasy at the reminder of his childhood curiosity: 'It was just a game; it was enough for a twelve-year-old, maybe, but it wasn't . . . finding out, you know; it wasn't *real*.' Yet the arrival above water of Leslie and Sarah is the parallel to the childhood Charlie. They are looking for somewhere to belong, despite the former ease of their everyday existence.

As Charlie finally emerges from his inertia, he discovers again the wonder of life and its sense of purpose and development. In his lengthy discussion of evolution the boundary between sea and air becomes a focus: 'What do they call it . . . the primordial soup? the glop? the heart-breaking second when it all got together, the sugars and the acids and the ultra-violets and the next thing you knew there were tangerines and string quartets.' Charlie explains to them all that they are part of the same wonderful process of life: 'there was a time when we were all down there, crawling around, and swimming and carrying on – remember how we read about it, Nancy . . .'

The sea–land exchange is crucial to Charlie's realisation that the four of them are united in all the implications of evolution from the 'aminos to the treble clef'.

> And do you know what happened once? Kind of the crowning moment of it all for me? It was when some . . . slimy creature poked its head out of the muck, looked around and decided to spend some time up here . . . came up into the air and decided to stay? And as time went on, he split apart and evolved and became tigers and gazelles and porcupines and Nancy here . . .
> LESLIE (*annoyed*): I don't believe a word of this!
> CHARLIE: Oh, you'd better, for he went back under, too; part of what he became didn't fancy it up on land, and went back down there, and turned into porpoises and sharks and manta rays, and whales . . . and you.

Charlie's vision includes them all as part of life and evolution. What is now vital is to know in what direction it is all going. Like the mirror couple they are, Leslie and

Sarah react in opposite directions. Sarah asks if it is all for the better, Leslie tells her not to be 'taken in'. By the end of the play Albee has revolutionised the situation at the outset. Faced with a carbon copy of his own and Nancy's attitudes, Charlie crusades to convince the neophytes of the possibilities that lie before them: 'What are you going to tell me about? Slaughter and pointlessness? Come on *up* here. *Stay.*'

Albee doesn't sentimentalise the play at this late point; the role of Charlie is to remain sceptical, Nancy hopeful, but the alteration is into awareness and commitment. The man has been stung into life by the conflict with the inhabitants of the sea he loved as a child. His sense of wonder is once more awakened. The ultimate development of this is in terms of the tensions which the theatre can produce. Albee shifts the conflict to the plane of emotions. The translation is apt in ideological terms. The commitment to life can only be achieved by the recognition of the emotions which are proof of one's reaction to existence. Charlie provokes a final confrontation as he makes Sarah weep at the suggested loss of Leslie, and Leslie in his turn react violently in defence of his mate. Charlie's motives are stated clearly for the audience to understand:

(*To* LESLIE *and* SARAH) I don't know what I want for *you*. I don't know what I feel toward you; it's either love or loathing. Take your pick; they're both emotions. And you're finding out about them, aren't you? About emotions? Well, I want you to know about *all* of it; I'm impatient for you, I want you to experience the whole thing! The full sweep!

As it stands, the play is concluded with the sea creatures coming to the arduous decision that they will stay on land when the painfulness of the experience they have been through seems too threatening. The final gestures of the play are touching but finally quite unsentimental as the quartet recognise in each other a necessary confrontation with life and the need to live. It is a choice that can be faced with, literally and figuratively, a helping hand. Hands and foot-paws are extended in the closing moments of the play. This conclusion contains the elements which resolve the questions and the experiences of the play, but nevertheless this work remains Albee's Unfinished Symphony. He has made it clear that there is a third act, which will complete the form of the play. As it stands, the play may seem slightly unbalanced, as the emphasis of discovery has shifted to the sea couple, and the ideas of wonder which are so joyously exposed in Nancy's speeches at the outset are overtaken by the development of relationships between the members of the oddly assorted quartet. This does work as a resolution of the action, for what is clearly and warmly felt by the audience is the primacy of life and genuine emotion in the play. However, one cannot help hoping that Albee will keep his promise to restore the final act, in which the positions are reserved and the human couple take up the theme of Charlie's childhood dreams and descend beneath the waves to discover life as something totally new, strange and fabulous.

The decision to shorten the play and abandon the third act indicates in part Albee's desire to keep its effect fully under control. The final act would have depended upon a theatrical dissolve into the underwater scene, which would have been very demanding technically but also visually stunning. The spectacle of the lizards would have gone much further, with submarine encounters with sea creatures, including a fight with an octopus. (In this Leslie would have rescued Nancy but Sarah would have died in coming to Nancy's assistance.) The scenic effects in the unpublished third act show, like *Tiny Alice*, Albee's power of imagination, and it is revealing that he should have decided to cut the fantastic episide which was to conclude the play.

> At a certain moment part of the play took place at the bottom of the sea. This was not necessary, it was too fantastic, and it was very difficult to realise a changeable set. Finally it was becoming a play centred on set changes.[35]

Albee's distrust of the merely decorative style of theatre against which he has struggled so energetically is revealed in this decision, and it supports the impression given by the present text of a play, which aims at a high degree of internal relevance and organisation of ideas and events. The extrapolation of the action into the third-act adventure would have been a justifiable pleasure for Albee to give himself as a writer. However, he has left the play now as a balance of the actual and the imagined in which the future is left to the audience and its reflection. The play therefore ends with an invitation: 'All right. Let's begin!' It is the positive image of the negative supplied in *All Over*, the companion play. That concludes with the end of a life and the eclipse of the possibility of change: 'All Over'.

8
Hermetic Albee: 'Listening'

In an interview in 1980 Albee spoke of 'a shift between hermetic and straightforward pieces'.

> I've been accused of becoming hermetic in my more recent work, and that my concern with language is getting a bit problematical for some people but that's just tough. They ignore the fact that some of my plays are absolutely straightforward and the next one will be hermetic and difficult. My last play which was called *Listening*, was commissioned by the BBC and done on radio, and was a fairly hermetic piece.[36]

The response was predictable. Val Arnold-Foster in *The Guardian* sensed its quality, but was still offended:

> It is undoubtedly well-written, tightly produced and immaculately acted, particularly by Irene Worth who brings all the warmth and emotional energy to the part of

the Woman that Albee demands of his performers. It is also so soggy with Symbolism and Significance that the play threatens to disappear into its mildly comic obscurity.[37]

Albee is remarkably uncompromising in his one radio play, where he has the opportunity of addressing a relatively large audience but still chooses not to adopt his 'straightforward' method.

On the other hand, the BBC commission gave him the chance of writing for a medium suited to his talent and corresponding to his fascination with the role of language in drama. He took up the challenge of writing experimentally: about listening. Beyond the stimulus of writing for the ears of his audience, Albee has adopted an inquiring attitude to the new medium. He here follows his own declared principles, articulated in the introduction to *Box* and *Quotations from Chairman Mao*:

> A playwright – unless he is writing escapist romances (an honourable occupation, of course) – has two obligations: first to make some statement about the condition of 'man' (as it is put) and, second, to make some statement about the nature of the art form with which he is working. . . . a playwright must try to alter the forms within which his precursors have had to work.

In *Listening* one can discern, through the hermetic methods, this articulation of a developing view of the human condition, and an attempt to deepen the view through a renewed understanding of the forms which can be attempted in the medium.

The play takes the form of a series of scenes introduced

by an external voice (in the first production this was the playwright's own), which calls a number. The method resembles the presentation, again by the playwright, of the scenes in *Box*. This 'intrusion' of the author's voice emphasises the role of the medium in shaping the experience of the listener. As the impression of the scene is established, the voice breaks in and numbers the items of the play; at one point the characters even debate the correctness of the numbering. While this involves the audience in the processes of constructing the play, the comfortable illusion is broken and the listener is aware of the play as a performance. Not real life – but intense and convincing.

Within the scenes Albee juxtaposes three characters: a man who seems to be arriving at a rendezvous; a woman who is a doctor or nurse, and who may have known the man in the past, and a girl who is the woman's charge. The scene is described in the opening reflections of the man as he awaits the meeting. It is the garden of an old house, a 'Man . . . si . . . on' which he imagines as having had in earlier times a private and personal use, whereas now it functions as an institution. The action takes place around an old dried-up fountain. A monstrous classical statue, possibly of a forgotten god, occupies the centre of the fountain, but the water is all gone and all that remains is a little green incrustration around the mouth.

Like *Box* this play evokes a nostalgia for, and sense of loss of, an earlier civilisation, represented by the physical setting: classical, Italian, French. Was it all brought over?, muses the Man:

All this was personal – long ago. Oh, turn of the century? or brought over – stone by stone, numbered, lettered, *mis*numbered, *mis*lettered? No question of it: personal,

131

once. Once. Once the walls were for the curious – to keep them *out*, when it was personal. And now they keep them *in*, do they not? The curious – the very curious, and the rest of us, the curious and the *less* curious.

The setting is implied: a sanatorium for the mentally ill. The characters are confined in an institution in a society which incarcerates the mentally curious. The feeling of a declining society and a lost culture accompanies the speculation that the whole edifice has been transported from another continent and wrongly re-erected. The underlying architectural base could be wrong. The images of the past are no longer clear; the 'God' cannot be identified; and the curious, those who wish to know about reality, are no longer free, but confined. The theme of madness has always had an attraction for Albee. In *The Zoo Story* and *Who's Afraid of Virginia Woolf?* the extremes of behaviour invite the question as to what, and which, is the 'sane' world: the private fantasy, or the vacuous society which is assumed to be real.

The reviewers who concluded that *Listening* was 'another' modern play about communication mistook Albee's interest in madness and the individual concept of reality. There is no problem of communication here: there is one in agreeing on what life is; in agreeing to share a reality and suffer it together. The relationships of the characters are never declared; what they have meant to one another in the past is never confirmed; and the stories they tell are questionable. The listener makes meanings as far as he may out of the words and sounds he hears; he constructs a reality – and is reminded that it is fictitious by the author's voice, or by what seem like cryptic remarks in the text:

THE MAN: Very much as promised. Great circular wall
   . . .
   Very much as stated. The marble pool . . .
   Very much as announced, indeed. All this . . .
   Very much as imagined . . . I would imagine.
   Very much as suggested, but . . .

The voice conveys the background to the action as
something created by the nature and methods of radio
broadcasting: promise, statement, announcement,
imagination and suggestion. The setting is never affirmed,
and the action is the result of a similar process of
suggestion. It is important to Albee's purpose that a sense
of reality arise out of the complex possibilities of the
interacting voices. There is no clear authorial fiction, but a
composition of speech actions. These achieve a sense of
reality through the convictions of the listener, not because
of the dominance of a verifiable story.

There is the simplest of narratives: a man is brought to a
girl by a woman who has promised to 'show him
something'. While the Woman watches the Girl, she
exchanges remarks which involve her ever more closely
with the Man. The two are drawn into an account of an
earlier encounter, and, as this brings the Woman to narrate
the suicide of a young woman, the Girl shows them that she
has cut her wrists. Besides this, the play is structured to
produce fragmentary indications of roles and relationships.
The Girl is a patient: she has relatives and a boy friend from
whom she once received visits, but latterly has withdrawn
into catatonia. She can be awakened from this by the snap
of the Woman's fingers. (The action recalls Beckett's
'mute' Lucky in *Waiting for Godot*, who is awakened into
thought by Pozzo.) The Woman is a nurse or possibly a
therapist, given control over the girl. She is aware of the

Girl as a case, and relates how she is disturbed, having attacked a fellow patient who laid hands on a prized piece of blue cardboard. The third character claims a relationship in the past with the Woman, and may be a cook in the institution. The Woman suggests he tell the Girl this as part of an attempt to persuade her to speak to him. His occupation may be fact, it may be invention, or it may be a private joke at the expense of the Girl's greed: merely a way of obtaining a response. Towards the end of the play, when the Man claims that he was once the Woman's lover, she dismisses *this* as invention and retorts with the gibe that he is merely a cook:

> THE MAN (*smiles*): I knew things *about* you; I knew *parts* of you.
> THE WOMAN (*a sad sneer*): You're a cook. It was lots of other people.
> THE MAN: What were they?
> THE WOMAN: You're a cook.
> THE MAN (*precise distaste*): I knew the things you liked – and I knew the things you pretended not to like, a longer list, by the way. Physical things, *and* ideas. I knew the phases of you.
> THE WOMAN (*precise distaste*): An 'institutional cook'.

The provoking inconsistencies of the accounts create Albee's characteristic sensation of loss. The Man recalls the ability of one to inflict pain on the other and tells how 'she' came to make him cry. The pain he experienced may be the evidence that there was a relationship, a reality that was shared. Weeping becomes an image in the lives of the three characters which indicates the intrusion of reality. The pain results from loss, the loss being the way in which real knowledge can be had of pleasure and the value of life.

The Woman gives her sad record of her losses, and the occasions when there was no loss to cry over:

> I cried the first time I realized someone had lied to me; I cried the first time I realized someone was trying very hard to be truthful; I cried the first time I had an orgasm, and I *didn't* cry the last time; you see? I told you: I cried at all the things; I cried when my parents died; I cried when my cats died; I cried when *I* . . . died.

The triangle is completed by the Girl, who is apparently the reason for the meeting of the other two; and who serves to unify and to bring to a climax the various accounts and ideas which are interwoven in the play. The exact relationships of the three characters are never to be known. They are linked by the communication of different perceptions of reality, and by the way in which these can be assembled in the process of performance. That the characters 'disagree' is not a matter of communication: to say this implies that reality is a matter of fact if the characters could only get through to one another. Albee's play depends upon articulate characters, presented by intelligent, thinking performers, and they communicate *too well* the fragments which potentially make an impression of what they hold on to and what they lack or have forgotten. The difficulty of the play is constructed, and has nothing to do with the portentous 'significance' that critics feel it is their mission to validate. The difficulty is the essential quality of the audience experience.

Albee plays with a quality of mind in the listener which builds patterns and relationships out of what is heard. He stimulates a penetrating sort of attention. In the play the Girl insists that the Woman lacks it:

THE GIRL: You don't *listen*.

THE WOMAN (*as if* THE MAN *were not there*). Well, that may *be*.

THE GIRL: Pay attention, rather, is what you don't do. Listen: oh, yes; carefully, to . . . oh, the sound an idea makes . . .

THE WOMAN: No, an *idea*.

THE GIRL (*thinks about it for a second*): Mmmmmmmmmmm . . . as the chemical thing happens, and then the electric thing, and then the muscle; *that* progression. The response – that almost reflex thing, the movement, when an idea happens.

Albee's style is opposed to the generalised performance and particularly to the projection of emotions, a vice which radio reveals as particularly inauthentic. Instead, the actor has a score to perform with great deliberation and mental exactness, but one which, if performed with the virtuosity all recognised in Irene Worth and the original cast, elicits a similar intense, sympathetic effort from the audience. The continuation of the sequence quoted above illustrates how Albee constantly requires a re-thinking of each *thought* (past), turning it into an idea (present):

THE MAN (*quiet awe*): Where does it come from?

THE WOMAN: What?

THE MAN: The . . . all that. Where does it come from?

THE WOMAN: I haven't found out. It all begins right there: she says, 'You don't listen.'

THE MAN: To what!? You don't listen to what!?

THE WOMAN (*sotto voce*): I don't *know* what I don't listen to.

THE MAN (*accusatory*): Yes, and do you care?

THE WOMAN (*so reasonable*): I don't *know*.

This is precise, but inconclusive. As with Pinter, Albee's fictions do not require verification. He does not aim at the illusion of a fixed past, but tries to create thinking and reacting in the present moment. This gives the listener the direct experience out of which the meanings of the play are built. At moments the significance of this process is made explicit. One such arises when the Woman tells the story of how her grandmother chose to end her life. As in *All Over* with its parallel description of the suicide of Dr Dey, Albee uses the image of death as the test for the value of life which is represented by the characters. The Woman's grandmother, she recalls, held that 'the greatest sin' was the waste of life in living it, and suicide, far from being waste, could be the point at which life was given significance and value. The important thing is 'taking your life in your own two hands'.

What matters is what can be done with life in the present, not what can be worked out over the long term. Acts are more important than conclusions. This explains the method. Albee aims at an immediate response which does not allow an easy reading to be built up steadily through the play. The play is structured to preserve a vitality of reaction, and at the same time Albee takes the risk that the audience's thinking will be strained when the story of his three characters does not emerge in familiar forms. The chain of action, motive and character may not be taken for granted. We hanker for the causal patterns of conventional realism, but this is not the way characters relate in this play:

THE WOMAN: You! You in the dress! Did I tell you she cried?
(THE GIRL *shakes her head; pauses, shakes it again, longer.*)

137

No? Well . . . yes. You hit her and she cried; cause and
    effect.

THE GIRL (*shakes her head*): No she didn't; I didn't see it,
    so it didn't happen: cause and effect.

THE WOMAN (*grudging admiration*): You *are* a *wonder!*
    Well, she did; she did cry. Does that make you feel
    anything?

THE GIRL (*as if discovering it for the first time*): Why is
    there no water?

Cause and effect are evoked in the strategic image of
characters crying. Tears are an indication of response,
and an invitation to share emotion. One knows the other
through pain: cause and effect. The Girl, described as
catatonic – thus clinically failing to respond to stimuli – is
crippled in her reactions. She challenges the Woman to
explain how she knows about the experience of others: the
demand is intensely defensive, as befits the withdrawn
position of the Girl. Tears are a test of reaction and she
refuses to admit to them. The Woman manifestly knows
about tears, for she describes her own up to the point where
she 'died' or became incapable of crying further. The Girl
becomes the focus for this talk of tears and reaction, for her
state is expressive of the connection Albee establishes
between the recognition of reality and the necessary
experience of pain. Thus the Woman details the wilful
refusal of the Girl to see her family any more and how she
resisted her natural reaction. This was the moment when
'she'd made it . . . to that awful plateau', ridding herself of
the people she might love; and, whatever the reaction
might have been, 'relief? pain?', it was stifled. This was the
moment 'she almost cried' and it would be the admission of
a human need. But to whom?

THE WOMAN: Well, without a soul to hear . . . why shouldn't she?

THE MAN (*feels dumb about saying it*): *You* were there.

THE WOMAN (*soft*, *ridiculing laugh*): Well. That's close enough; I don't exist, you know.

Acts such as these produce a complex resonse. Reduced to any simplified fiction their effect is lost. Does or did the Woman exist? What does she mean by claiming that she does not exist? Should we understand this as a reference to her own withdrawal, to the 'death' she speaks of elsewhere? Her words suggest a state which parallels the psychosis of the Girl, who in return claims that it is *she* who does not exist.

Interpretation allows a partial rendering of the expressive possibilities of the text, but at the same time it is a betrayal. Ambiguities are of a piece with the sensations of loss, isolation and crisis created by the performance. Was there anyone to hear the Girl? If the narrative is 'true', then it is also true that the narrator was elsewhere, or does not exist. Yet she exists to tell the story in which these contradictions arise. *Listening* has its climax in a parallel ambiguity: the Girl achieves the suicide which the Woman at the outset claims she will prevent, and yet the Woman implies she knows that it is taking place. The danger is foreshadowed in the references to 'the guile' with which the Girl would take 'sharp glass' were there any in the fountain. The Woman declares that such is her attention that she would judge from the Girl's responses that there was a cutting edge to hand. The Girl finds something or has brought something (she does not specify) and yet the Woman calmly insists that she *listens*, and has in some way watched the suicide attempt take place.

The effect of performance is to suggest that the Woman

cares, but accepts the suicide. She demands 'with concern' to know if there is anything in the fountain with the Girl. The listener can also hear the moment of decision in the Girl's performance, although it cannot be registered as a specific event. 'Why live?' asks the Woman, and the Man shrugs in reply, 'Indeed', echoed softly by the Girl. When the Man interrupts the Woman he is again echoed by the Girl – 'All right!' – and then, as the Woman begins a story about blood, the Girl repeats, as though 'acquiescing to something' the same words, but with a change of emphasis. The listener can hear the decision but the significance becomes explicit only as the Woman looks back: 'There was something, then.' This dislocation whereby an impression of an event has confirmation elsewhere, or indeed re-emerges only half-remembered or acknowledged, is the heart of the play. Albee creates an experience of the tension between the risk of reality and the pain of withdrawal. In order to arouse his listener, Albee writes against the grain of the causation we take for granted and adds to the play a pattern of significant images which link one set of sensations with another. The action is dislocated, the sensations are not directly connected, one arising from another; but out of the composition there arises a sensation of need and of risk and of loss.

The use of a psychotic state establishes a pattern of response with the play. According to the stage direction, the Girl 'withdraws into herself', and in this state her relationship to the outside world is problematic: is she a butterfly as the man thinks, or a praying mantis? The mention of another girl patient in the sanatorium allows an intensification of the feeling of isolation and the destruction of the relationships surrounding the individual. There is both destruction and suffering in the account of her desire for 'reality':

THE WOMAN: She climbed the stair; she took the baby
from the crib, she took it by the ankles . . .

THE MAN: No! Please!

THE WOMAN: Took it by the ankles and bashed its head
against the wall. I suppose that gained a *little* more
reality; I don't know.
(*Pause.*)
She's a sad girl.

Both girls have violently rejected a reality which seemed
'too little' and withdrawn into catatonia. This rejection of
the everyday is familiar in Albee, although it does not occur
elsewhere in quite such gruesome images.

Listening goes further than any other play in trying to
explore the sensation of isolation within the self. This is
equivalent to the fantasy life of George and Martha with
their son, but that is a shared experience capable of
generating feelings of understanding and support. Here
Albee writes for the unsupported individual, as he had
done more simply in his first play, *The Zoo Story*. Both
women in the play state at certain points that they do not
exist, and assert that the other one does. The play plainly
raises the question of what existence is like and at what
points the individual is conscious of living; hence the
Woman's assertion that she 'died' at some time in the past,
and the association of faint memories with the suggestion of
life: the fountain filled, the Woman with 'one of her beaux'.
What really survives is the recollection of the times she
cried, all moments of intense recognition of the reality of
living.

Equally the Girl in her withdrawn state has been seen
actually to cry and she herself is the cause of it. She cries
when she menstruates.

THE WOMAN: She bleeds; once a month she bleeds, and she cries: the phases of the moon. God, every woman from the dawn of time . . .

THE GIRL (*teeth clenched; intense*): I am the only one.

This is a bitter encounter between the Girl and the Woman. All three characters challenge one another over questions of identity and the truth of their different accounts of themselves. In this particular revelation Albee invests the account of the Girl crying at the sight of her own blood with a special power. He creates a subtle linking of ideas (for they are thought through) to stand side by side with the imperfect chain of cause and effect in the play. To a certain extent it is possible, and tempting, to speak of a pattern of images, for some of the ideas which are linked and recur have an independent imaginative life, and a visual power. Albee uses his ideas, however, as an integral part of the dramatic structure, carefully engineering their use so that they reappear and recombine in what is poetically a highly suggestive fashion. It is once more an illustration of what he means by his musical style of writing. In this play one can best speak of *themes* in a musical sense, and understand the development of themes as with a composer, the reappearance and the modification of the theme growing out of the compositional structure and owing its placing to the hand of the composer.

In this fashion Albee establishes a relationship between the three accounts of tears which bring the characters into conflict, and a theme of blood which comes to dominate the last part of the play. The Man understands the tears which the Girl sheds and asks who would not. The withdrawn girl resolutely insists that she is the only one to bleed. Both of them agree that blood is 'the colour of pain', with the strong overtone that the pain is most acute in the isolation and

142

physical experience of the self. The Woman takes up the theme and implies another attitude not based on the fear. She rejects the insistence on blood as pain, certainly in the sense that they offer. She affirms its part in life:

> I take pain as a warning, not a punishment; it's information; what's wrong with all you people?
> THE MAN (*quiet irony*): Much, I dare say.
> THE WOMAN: Everything scares us – prolapse, blood, the heartbeat . . . Why live!?

Blood entails the confrontation with the physical reality of the self, as does the other crucial encounter remembered by the Man as having been shared with the Woman, and which, consistent with the structuring of the action, she disputes. He asserts that he has known her intimately including her 'phases' (taking up the term the Woman uses to refer to the Girl's menstruation). He goes further. He remembers how she turned her face from his in their lovemaking because she could not accept her sexuality: 'you must have thought I was going to kiss you, my mouth from your cunt become a cunt, a cunt descending on your mouth, yours on your mouth'. From him this was the sign of his rejection; the time she caused him to cry in his isolation. Albee merges his themes as the Man insists on knowing the reason the Woman turned away:

> THE WOMAN (*offhand*): Was it *you*?
> THE MAN: Was it because I had no blood on my mouth?

Albee uses the resonance of the ideas he has been developing to suggest both the particular physical facts of this remembered encounter *and* the accumulated implications: blood, pain and isolation. Reflecting on how

143

she averted her face, the Man muses on how most actually want *just* their own reality even in love: to be the subject and the object at the same time in the act of love. 'We all love ourselves and wish we could.' His reaction to the woman in the past, if it was the Woman, suggests that he failed. Would he avoid her menstrual blood? Why, as he cried over her, did he masturbate? The suggestion is that avoidance and isolation were on his side.

Blood leads to the simultaneous narrative of the conclusion, recalled through thoughts of blood, and the girl's calm suicide. The story the Woman tells describes an encounter with, again, a psychotic girl, with 'the detached voice' she has since come to know well. The girl's conversation she recalls as having no thread. Like the forms of the play itself it is 'nonsequential . . . probably the most difficult to adjust to'. True to the nonsequential method, this narration includes details which point back to the play. The Girl in the story offers to 'show her somethng' – which recalls the motive for the summoning of the Man at the outset. Recognising the girl's state, the Woman was not 'going to be surprised' at what might result; perhaps there might be a dead baby, recalling the earlier story of the 'sad girl' who killed her child. Nor is the Woman surprised in her story when the girl draws her hands from her pockets 'filled with her blood'. As the Woman demonstrates, the Girl quietly echoes the story by offering them her bleeding wrists. The story and the final image synthesise elements which are carefully composed over eighty minutes or so of playing time. The Man sees 'something' as promised, and ironically Albee gives him the word again as he cries, 'Do something! Something!' Suicide may also be 'the one thing . . . that matters'. The suicide is felt as something terrible, and yet, like the death of the Woman's grandmother, something which belongs to a 'proper' understanding of life. In no way can we suggest a naturalistic interpretation of Albee's action in *Listening*: the *Woman* does not bring the Man to see a suicide, yet, as has been seen, she is aware and chooses not to prevent the Girl as she cuts her wrists. If it is decided that the Man was her lover, has Albee simply cursed his heroine with a bad memory and so on?

Throughout the play Albee exploits the natural capacity of the listener to build patterns, and this involves the narrative sense. In order to play with the listener's imagination, Albee interposes memory between his characters and adds the altered perspective of schizophrenia. Memory allows the location of characters in past time, or their removal as the composition requires. For example, the sexual relationship of the Man and the Woman is allowed a greater possibility of interaction by her amused reaction to his sexual descriptions: 'No; a temporal being! It's not the *way* you think of things. "I have a temporal being." I think I recognize you; I saw you cry once.' She accepts that she might have known him; if she did it was she who made him cry; but he maintains she did not *see* him cry. The memories create possibilities to be played out, but they are not reliable when they seem to be making probable links. Similarly, the withdrawn perspective of the Girl constructs a private reality; as the Woman asks her patient, 'What you see is invented by your seeing it?'

For some listeners this method may prove provoking, as the writer refuses to create a story (Albee might call it a romantic fiction) and turn the past into a deep-frozen piece of reality. Like Pinter, Albee writes games to be played with the themes of past time. He may conceivably owe a debt to his fellow dramatist, whose methods are so comparable in *Old Times*, where, similarly, two women and a man grapple with the possibilities of their

145

relationship. Kate, a character similar in her remoteness to the Girl, is partnered by her husband, Deeley, and her old friend Anna. The different accounts of their interactions in the past do not tally, playing out the potential of different pairings, without allowing a conclusive account to prevail. As Anna revealingly remarks, 'There are things which I remember which may never have happened but as I recall them so they take place.'[38] No less than Pinter, Albee is sensitive to the suggestive power of drama, and in *Listening* the shifting, unreliable texture of the writing allows the suggestion of potential rather than presenting a massive and unalterable structure of cause and effect. *Listening* is probably Albee's most hermetic piece, and certainly is as musical in its impact as it is complex and intellectually stimulating. It is also an important play for the demonstration of the freedom and exploration which is characteristic of his play-writing. Hermetic Albee casts light on the dramatist at his more straightforward.

9
'The Lady from Dubuque'

The Lady from Dubuque was expected to be a play in the mould of *Who's Afraid of Virginia Woolf?* Indeed, the project was conceived at the same time that the earlier play was gestating in Albee's imagination in 1960. Over the years Albee spoke of plans for incorporating a singularly ambitious effect, an enormously extended speech; but this was abandoned. So too was the title by which the project was first known: 'The Substitute Speaker'. When the play was performed in 1980 it recalled the 'early' Albee: the idea of substitution contained in the original title, and the presence of what the writer called 'hallucinatory' elements, both suggesting affiliation to *Who's Afraid of Virginia Woolf?* The play retained the economy of Albee's later writing, and the non-naturalistic experiments were distinctly the fruit of his confidence in his style, abundantly displayed in the two plays *Counting the Ways* (1976) and *Listening* (1975). At the same time the twenty-year-old project emphasised the continuity of some of Albee's most expressive dramatic ideas.

147

The setting is familar: the suburban surroundings, the middle-class socialising, the atmosphere of depression and decline, and, through the alcoholic haze, the games people play. His ability to use the cliché or the innocent phrase to suggest hidden malaise is just as striking. The blandness and the very weariness of the game-playing creates a surface through which the rifts can momentarily be glimpsed. The rituals of hospitality and friendship, and even the support of marriage, are minutely dismantled to reveal their motive forces. The opening image of the play, the assembled party playing Twenty Questions, poses innocently the one question which the characters avoid: 'Who am I?' The action presents them with a character whose identity is in turn the question upon which the action hinges. And, when the newcomer eventually replies to their tormented questioning, her response is grotesque: 'Why, I'm the Lady from Dubuque. I thought you knew.' The most vital question is answered with a joke: a character from the *New Yorker*'s 'Talk of the Town' column: the mythical, unsophisticated little old lady from the mid-West for whom the magazine's founder said he would distinctly not be catering. She is an invention. The title of the play suggests matters of value rather than structure (as, say, in *A Delicate Balance* or *All Over*). It is clear that the stranger, Elizabeth, is a 'substitute speaker' and a necessary invention. In the midst of the ease and affluence which represents the material dimension of the American Dream, the social group is shown to be desiccated and barren. None of them mentions children. One of them needs a mother. Albee invents her.

Four assorted couples meet in the play. Six of the characters comprise a group of apparently good friends who are discovered enjoying one of their regular parties. On this occasion it is in the home of Jo and Sam. The group appears stable and in every way unremarkable, and it is this appearance which the play is designed to undermine. The arrival of a fourth couple, an elegant middle-aged woman and her sophisticated black companion, exposes a destructive potential in the group, in a manner which inverts the arrangement of *Who's Afraid of Virginia Woolf?* In this play the guests, uninvited, get the hosts. The paradox which the play creates arises from the fact that Jo, the central character, forms a more natural relationship with the enigmatic woman visitor than she has with anyone else, including her husband. Jo sees events quite differently from her group and this creates significant tensions in the action. She differs in another important respect, and there is an implied connection: she is dying of cancer. Although she is surrounded by her husband and friends, and although she is in her home, she lacks support, as she says, 'IN THE HOUR OF MY GODDAM NEED'. The unknown strangers supply the support. Elizabeth and Oscar are the names they are given. But to the end they remain unidentifiable. It is suggested that Elizabeth is Jo's mother, but she is not. Oscar is demonstrably not her husband, but this does not prevent Jo, at one time, from seeing him in this role. And 'role' is the key. The excitement and the beauty of Albee's play lies in the way he digs into the unquestioned relationships which make a life, and realigns his characters, not in terms of what or who they are assumed to be, but in terms of what they do. Those who have a clear identity have a less clear purpose and role in life. Thus the question 'Who am I?', 'Who are you?'

The play was not a popular success. In *Who's Afraid of Virginia Woolf?* the abundance of verbal invention disguised the boldness of Albee's invention. Although audiences were mystified by the idea of an imaginary child, the uneasiness was swept away by the force of the writing.

Edward Albee

In *The Lady from Dubuque* there is an equivalent problem of a mother who is unreal according to definitions articulated in the play. However, the refinement of Albee's style makes the inconsistencies of the action clearer and more challenging to the audience. Rather like Harold Pinter, Albee employs a technique of limited abstraction to unsettle the predictable response to the stage. The representation of reality is familiar enough up to a point where Albee detaches and enhances key actions. This is done simply and without justification, resulting in a clear tension with the naturalistic flow of the play elsewhere. It is ironic that writing of this sort, which affirms the part of the audience in constructing its meanings, should be less warmly received than his earlier works on the grounds of its ambiguity. Albee's critics and audiences did not, for the most part, share his view that the play was 'straightforward', for straightforwardness in some eyes does not admit a complex understanding of reality.

The subject of the play is Jo's dying, and the treatment differs notably from the other obvious 'death' play, *All Over*. In both works the act of dying challenges the values of life in different characters; in both plays Albee explores his idea of death as important not as a state but as a process. However, in this work he seems acutely sensitive to the experience of death itself: he places the sufferer at the centre of the action and concentrates on her crisis, then he locates the arrival of Elizabeth and Oscar prominently at the act change 'in time' for Jo's last agony. There is a preparation and the dying.

The appearance of stability and even boredom which is given at the outset of the play is rapidly destroyed by the intrusion of Jo's pain. The uneasy rituals of Sam and Jo's gang are unbalanced when they have to be measured against the need and the coming death of one among them.

The Lady from Dubuque

Manners begin to disintegrate as the meaning of relationships is exposed. Edgar protests at Jo's treatment of his wife Luscinda:

> She says she can't take it any more, Jo, the way you go on at her; the way you make such terrible fun of her in front of everybody! She says it was all right until you got sick but now you're sick you mean it in a different way, and it's breaking her heart.

Jo's pain alters everything. It exposes her relationships with others; her dislike for Luscinda, and her admiration for Carol, who is not deceived in the compromise she makes in her partnership with the 'blond ex-athlete' Fred. As the evening breaks down, the characters declare themselves, answering the essential Twenty Questions:

JO: Who *are* you, Carol?
CAROL (*stretches*): Ooooooh, I'm a lady of parts; I got facets, too, you know.

In addition to the pressure exerted by Jo's sickness, the games the friends play have their own inner tensions. The players are locked in. As Fred says, with the stage direction 'stern', 'Wives play; girl friends play; everybody plays.' Albee's enjoyment is evident in creating the underlying feelings of animosity and irritation which accompany the playing. There is a counterpoint between the level of the game, and the level of the more significant interactions which accompany it. As Sam tries to sustain the game, the character of the group emerges:

EDGAR: Are you a man?
SAM: No.
JO: Coulda fooled *me*.

CAROL (*to* FRED): Then he's a woman.

FRED: Of course he's a woman! What the fuck do you think he is!

CAROL (*getting angry*): He could be a dog, or a horse, or something!

FRED: A horse!? What do you mean, a horse? Nobody's ever been a horse! You're always embarrassing me!

CAROL: I'm trying to learn the game! You want me to fit in, don't you? Well? Besides, what's embarrassing about a horse?

JO (*as if the question were to be answered*): What's embarrassing about a horse? Well, let's see . . .

Inevitably the tensions of the group turn the games into ritual conflicts. Their damaging potential is developed further as the private games of individual relationships are implicated. The first clear rift between Jo and Sam appears when she is successful in guessing who he is in Twenty Questions. He is not one person but two: Romulus and Remus. She guesses because he has extended a private game she remembers when he took her breast, saying he was Romulus and Jo the she-wolf. Two reactions are striking. Sam is exposed and lightly victimised by his friends; and he continues the game, playing for them the role of Romulus. Amid the kidding and barracking, he admits that he killed Remus; he speculates about his jealousy for him, and wonders if he took his favourite teats.

Out of this sort of dramatic game-playing Albee extracts his old blend of disturbingly ineffective and inauthentic action. The celebrations which accompany Sam's victory in the game are led by Edgar with 'not much enthusiasm'; and the forms of action are commented on by Jo: 'Sam wins. I guess it, and Sam wins.' Jo's glum reflection on the justice of the game evolves into a more bitter dissatisfaction: at least Sam, having the she-wolf, had a mother. He is 'curiously annoyed' at this development in the game. The audience has no way of knowing when the game ends, and what takes its place:

> SAM: You've got a perfectly good mother!
> JO (*clearly this is a private argument*): Yeah? Where is she? Where the hell is she?
> SAM (*spits it out*): 'In the hour of your need?'
> JO (*hard*): YEAH! IN THE HOUR OF MY GODDAM NEED!

The game leads to the essential question: has Jo a mother, if she is not present in her daughter's hour of need? The drift from one sort of contest to another allows Albee to put the question without the audience being aware of how ambiguous a character Jo's mother is to prove. What seems to be is not dependable. The ambivalence of events at large is worked out in an extended game, in fact a play within the play, concocted to amuse the company; and in it Albee subverts the audience's safe perspective on what is 'serious' and what is 'fun'. Sam and Carol return to the stage midway through the first act. Carol accuses Sam of molesting her in the bathroom. The game produces significant reactions: Lucinda is thrilled, Edgar curious; and Fred prepares for battle:

> FRED (*getting to his feet; belligerent*): OK. now, just what the fuck's going –
> CAROL (*a sudden imitation of a violated maiden; falsetto*): Fred? Would you take me home please? I've been vastly insulted!
> FRED (*ready for battle now*): You're fuckin – A right I will! Jesus Christ, Sam!
> *But* CAROL *and* SAM *have dissolved into laughter, are hanging on to each other for support.*

When Fred realises he has been fooled he is disarmed and revealed. He knows they have learned something about him with his 'clothes off', but, more important, he may have learned something about himself. Jo with a 'half-smile' of recognition asks why he did not hit anyone. He seems to have acted out of character: belligerent but not violent. His reply is an ingenuous statement which exposes his real involvement with the group: maybe he likes them.

The games elicit the unstated relationships of the characters. The bystanders are just as involved. Luscinda tries to find her place in the game, without an idea of its implication, and in silencing her Edgar betrays the weight of his hostility to her. Fred is robbed of his protective masculinity by the fiction Carol invents. When the game ceases he finds he cannot take his role for granted. It is not 'like him' not to strike out. He is at the same time exposed and forced to take stock. What is he? What *is* he like?

This precariousness of identity is underlined by one of the basic techniques Albee adopts in drawing attention to the theatre medium. While he develops a more or less uninterrupted stream of action on the stage, he withdraws performers to make a direct address to the audience. The fiction proceeds, but the actor or actress invites a judgement or shares a point of view. Albee does not ask the performer to abandon the role (as he does in *Counting the Ways*), and the characterisation of a role such as Jo's is in fact further developed through the device. It is on the other hand a way of breaking down the naturalistic interpretation of performance. It is an extention of the tradition of the aside, and allows a more detailed presentation of the actions and reactions which occur within a given role. The technique disturbs a certain comfortable enjoyment of fiction in the theatre, but the disturbance is a way of showing the values in the action we watch. If the style of characterisation undermines expectations, this is clearly relevant to a play which persistently articulates the question 'Who am I?'

The relationship of actor and audience is never assumed to be constant, and is exploited in a variety of ways. Initially it may seem that Albee casts the audience as *confidant* to the character. This is the case at the outset when Jo upstages the rest of the cast mischievously with her disparaging interventions: 'Don't you just hate party games? Don't you just hate them?' As the strains grow more evident, the audience is treated as watchers who expose action to the general view. Sam's embarrassment before the group is amplified by calling attention to the audience:

> JO (*to the audience; a little rueful herself*): Death's door and all. *And* . . . he had one of my breasts, and he was sort of bouncing it around a little . . .
> FRED (*to* SAM): You debbil!
> JO (*still to the audience*): . . . and he started nibbling, and then he started sucking . . .
>> (*to* SAM) . . . which breast was it, Sam?
> SAM (*embarrassed, therefore cold*): I don't recall: I was occupied.
>> (*Refers to the audience.*) For God's sake, Jo!

This is technically difficult for the performers. They have to sustain concentration within the stage environment, and from time to time accept the watching audience as part of their circumstances. On the other hand it does produce quite an original effect, since the cutting process aims at increasing the emotional intensity and consistency of the playing. The difficulty of the process is the condition for its success. With his instinct for the medium Albee searches out the effects and tensions of performance. He uses the vulnerability of performers and audience alike which results from the blurring of the conventions and demarcation lines in the theatre, and that vulnerability is felt as a real presence. The resulting tension becomes significant within a play which attempts to maintain a strained ambivalent response to identity. This ambivalence of the characters – do we see them in a play, or in a theatre? – is highly necessary in introducing the two strangers who arrive at the painful crisis of Act I, as Jo's illness develops. They arrive with a declared intention in the action, but they enter effectively from the theatre, not within the set:

> ELIZABETH *and* OSCAR *enter the set from one side, from without the set.* OSCAR *is dressed in a suit and tie.* ELIZABETH *is dressed elegantly.* ELIZABETH *sees the audience, puts her finger to her lips, lest* THEY *start commenting, or applauding, or whatever.*

> OSCAR (*looking about, with some distate*): You say this is the place?
> ELIZABETH (*to the audience, not urgent, not languid, but no nonsense*): Is she alive? Are we here in time?
>> (*The sound of* JO's *screams from upstairs; a brief silence, then another scream*).
> ELIZABETH (*still in the audience, her eyes acknowledging the sound with a brief upward movement of her head*): Ah yes! Well, then; we *are* in time.
>> (*Turns her head slightly toward* OSCAR.) Yes; this is the place.

The curious reference to the audience as 'THEY' gives a clue to Albee's intention. His spectators are to be engaged onlookers, but in an event whose significance goes beyond the suburban narrative and the imagined last illness of a fictitious character. The importance of Albee's stylistic experiments is in riveting attention on performance where the quality of the experience is to do with the actual states witnessed and the ideas and thinking which are considered. In this play the links which unite the roles are not susceptible to the forms of naturalistic theatre which presuppose a certain view of the everyday relationships of persons. In such a theatre there is one answer to the question of who is Jo's mother. It is a matter of fact. In Albee's play it is a matter of function.

The appearance of Elizabeth and her companion replies to the ambiguous or contradictory remarks which are made in the first act about Jo's mother. The two newcomers furthermore suggest a play of relationships which contrast with the life of Jo's group. The strangers are a source of security to the dying woman, where her friends and husband had been threatened by her illness. There is a symmetry between the two acts which is developed to bring out the quasi-musical possibilities of the writing. The games of the first act appear as variations in the second. Oscar and Elizabeth reply to Sam's desperate and very natural question, 'Who are you?' by turning the question back on him, and the game of Twenty Questions is on. The phrases of the opening of the play reappear linked to the question, 'Was she my mother?' and establish the question which is central in the new formulation: is Elizabeth Jo's mother? As the game is played we can judge that Sam looks for the ordinary credentials in a person, while Albee writes to establish identity through what one person does for another. Elizabeth nursed a sick woman once; much as she now comes in time or the crisis in Jo's illness. What mattered was the nursing, and the identity of the woman is of minor consequence.

ELIZABETH (*this speech to both* SAM *and the audience*): I remember someone, a lady who had been good to me, a lady much older than I, older than I am now and I was young; I remember there was no one else to do it all; it was on *me*; I didn't like any of it: injecting, swabbing, bathing, changing, holding close, holding her close to crush the pain out of her . . .

(*To* SAM *alone now*) I wonder who she was? Was she my mother? I hope you're prepared for it.

SAM (*finally*): WHO *ARE* you!!!???

ELIZABETH (*so calm*): You're shouting. Who *am* I?

(*To the audience*) The gentleman wants to know who I am.

(*To* SAM) Well . . . who are you?

SAM: I'm Jo's husband; this is my house . . .

Sam's answer takes us back to the opening game in the play. The words describe property rights, what belongs to him; and this is the way in which his group identifies itself. Elizabeth and Oscar put the question in different terms. Playing their ridiculous game as 'house inspectors', they provoke Sam as to their identity, and then in the same breath turn the question on him.

This invasion brings with it a strange new way of looking at people. As Sam fulminates, Oscar and Elizabeth calmly discuss their watching in the night. He rarely sleeps, she dozed a little, 'watched the night die'; but what did Sam *do*? Identity is the fruit of action. Elizabeth and Oscar have heard the cries in the night and ask if Sam has done his part:

ELIZABETH (*to* SAM): Did *you* sit up? We heard the cries, and then the silence. Did you sit up, and hold her hand until the drugs had done their work? Did you lie down beside her then, put off the light, and stare up into the dark?

The Lady from Dubuque

Sam's notion of rights crumbles before Elizabeth's proven effectiveness in the home. He assumes a regulated situation in which he leads his life, and this is cruelly altered as all the old rules break down. When he demands that Fred leave, his friend punches him in the stomach, an act which is all the more violent and unrestrained since Sam has been tied up by Oscar. When Carol announces she will do as she pleases too, and stay behind after Fred for a cup of coffee, Fred spontaneously smashes the cups and saucers. The recognition of the true relationship of the friends is complete when Luscinda and Edgar walk out, the man passionately complaining, 'I'm not here, God damn you!' He has no rights and his mere existence is not truly acknowledged. This is a crisis which arises from the insufficiency of the group: the strangers are used to dramatise the implications of the hollowness of its commitment and the emptiness of its gestures of comradeship. Elizabeth and Oscar have no duties and no entitlement but they assume the key functions beside Jo. The fact that the two remain critically detached from the action, and yet vitally affect its course, is a direct realisation of the absence of value in the internal relationships of the play. An absent mother's place is filled by one whose ability to bring comfort identifies her sufficiently. The question is not whether Elizabeth is Jo's mother, for it becomes clear with time that secure identifications are irrelevant to Jo's needs. The intruders show in action the human capacity that Jo's circle exhibit only by its absence. Thus Jo progressively recognises and interacts with characters who are from different points of view enigmatic, or fantastic.

The device allows Albee to dramatise some particularly moving effects. The culmination of Jo's agony is treated with great compassion as she regresses into childhood and is cared for accordingly. There is a direct contrast: at the close of the first act Sam described as 'helpless' struggles to help Jo upstairs; in the second, Oscar 'scoops' her up in his arms while speaking similar lines: 'I'll take care of you now; I'll make you better; you'll see; I'll put you right to bed; I'll make you better . . .'

Jo's relationship with her 'real' husband depends upon games. In the first act the fact of her death and its consequences for Sam emerge as she demands, 'Come on! Play!' And the game produces the suggestion that Sam will marry Carol after her death, the woman with whom he plays his charade; and who remains almost to the final moments of the play, releasing Sam as her final act. In a complex fashion the relationship of Sam and Jo needs the ability to 'play' and in this certain truths appear. When the real test comes with her pain, Jo 'waves him off'. Sam is the 'good man' of the opening games, but he cannot cope with the stark reality of his wife's death. Death, that is to say reality, is the real intruder in this play.

Albee takes risks in the way he develops the dramatic possibilities of this intrusion. When Oscar assumes Sam's role, he also takes up the same stage position and adopts his lines. There is an absurd side to Oscar's performance, verging on a parody of Sam. Soon after his arrival Oscar suggests he might be a relative, and when Sam rejects this he forces Sam to admit that he cannot be *like* him – because he is black. Oscar's amusement at Sam's discomfiture is no less when he appears impersonating him wearing his nightshirt. But under this fooling Oscar plays his role for real: the direct converse of those whose social shell is convincing and who are betrayed by their actions. In the essential functions of comforter and friend, Oscar has a compassion Sam cannot find. As Oscar lightly carries Jo upstairs, Albee directs the players to evoke a *pietà*. Earlier Sam asks the strangers if they have no compassion; this is his answer. The stranger is able to discharge the function of the husband. There is more than an echo of Albee's Angel of Death in *The Sandbox*, where another death is treated with special compassion by the playwright.

The dramatic method has the effect of widening the significance of the theme of death. For the individuals it entails the realisation of the limits of their response one to another. The use of the abstract characters of Elizabeth and Oscar places the question in a still larger perspective. They demand nothing and defend no position. While being thoroughly integrated in the action, they can also assume the role of the chorus in classical drama and register the larger emotional values, and the wider context of significance. Not only does Elizabeth express movingly the pity of Jo's death; she is the means of affirming the essential values of life. When she tells the story of her upbringing in Iowa, Elizabeth recalls her understanding of the most important question: 'Who am I?' Sam in reply confesses he does not know who he is. Albee's meanings become clearer within the dimension of American society, 'the last democracy' at the point where it confronts the possible death of its civilisation.

In the last moments of the play Sam regresses to a 'shivering little boy' and asks Elizabeth's assurance that the end of things will be silent 'with no time to be afraid'. She tells a dream of dying, and in it he recognises the death of the world in a nuclear age: 'We knew what we were watching, and there was no time to be afraid. The silence was . . . beautiful as the silent bombs went off.' Elizabeth's words bring comfort to a dying society, but it is one whose values are infantile. She makes the images of a peaceful end; she also provides an abstract example of commitment and self-awareness which might make a society capable of confronting the challenges of self-destruction. The shadow of 'mushroom doomsday' is cast over the play from the outset, and then the issues are transformed into Albee's familiar brew of the personal and the significant. Underneath there is perhaps his clearest affirmation of the political commitment in his writing. What the play seems to have lacked is the ability, so richly evident in the raw energy of *Who's Afraid of Virginia Woolf?*, to provoke an audience. The confrontational attitude is replaced by a method which creates more precisely the forms in which the dramatist can play upon the audience's responses. Although the play is far from difficult and contains much that is immediately funny or affecting, it is experimental in its form and moves the dramatist ever further from the realistic traditions of American theatre. It also tries to do this with a public whose taste is formed by the visual naturalism of television and cinema. *The Lady from Dubuque* requires a degree of theatrical sophistication not to be expected of the Lady from Dubuque.

Notes

1. Ruby Cohn, *New American Dramatists*, (London: Macmillan, 1982) p. 5.

2. Preface to *The American Dream*.

3. Interview in Michael E. Rutenberg, *Edward Albee: Playwright in Protest* (New York: DBS Publications, 1969) pp. 231–2. Albee refers to Rose Zimbardo, 'Symbolism and Naturalism in Edward Albee's *The Zoo Story*, *Twentieth Century Literature*, 8, no. 1 (Apr 1962).

4. Interview in Rutenberg, *Albee: Playwright in Protest*, p. 247.

5. *New York Times*, 28 March 1976.

6. *New York Times*, 18 Feb 1963.

7. *Los Angeles Times*, 27 Dec 1964.

8. Digby Diehl, 'Edward Albee Interviewed', *Transatlantic Review* no. 13 (Summer 1963) p. 72.

9. *New Yorker*, 19 Dec 1964.

10. Quoted in Anita Maria Stenz, *Edward Albee: The Poet of Loss* (The Hague: Mouton, 1978) p. 55, n. 15.

11. Tom F. Driver, 'What's the Matter with Edward Albee', *The Reporter*, 2 Jan 1964.

12. Diehl interview, *Transatlantic Review*, no. 13, pp. 71–2.

13. *Pittsburgh Press*, 3 Feb 1974.

14. *New York Times*, 30 July 1967.

15. *New York Times*, 18 Apr 1971.

16. Charles Marowitz (ed.), *New American Drama* (London: Penguin, 1966) p. 11.

17. *New York Herald Tribune*, 3 Oct 1971.

18. Interview in Rutenberg, *Albee: Playwright in Protest*, p. 298.

19. August Strindberg, *Letters to the Intimate Theatre*, tr. Walter Johnson (London: Peter Owen, 1967) p. 19.

20. *Saturday Review*, 24 Jan 1970.

21. *Newsweek*, 4 Feb 1963.

22. *San Francisco Chronicle*, 12 Oct 1978.

23. *Washington Post*, 26 Mar 1967.

24. Interview in Rutenberg, *Albee: Playwright in Protest*, p. 235.

25. Marowitz (ed.), *New American Drama*, p. 11.

26. C. W. E. Bigsby, *Albee* (Edinburgh: Oliver and Boyd, 1969) p. 69.

27. *Saturday Review*, 30 Jan 1965.

28. *New York Times*, 27 Dec 1964.

29. Strindberg, *Letters to the Intimate Theatre*, p. 132.

30. *Women's Wear Daily*, 8 Oct 1973.

31. *New York Times*, 23 May 1978.

32. Interview in Rutenberg, *Albee: Playwright in Protest*, p. 230.

33. *New York Times*, 28 March 1976.

34. Stenz, *Albee: The Poet of Loss*, p. 115.

35. *New York Times*, 21 Jan 1975.

36. Interview with Peter Adam, *The Listener*, 7 Feb 1980.

37. *The Guardian*, 27 Mar 1976.

38. Harold Pinter, *Old Times* (London: Methuen, 1971) pp. 31–2.

Bibliography

Plays by Edward Albee

The Zoo Story, *The Death of Bessie Smith*, *The Sandbox* (New York: Coward McCann, 1960).

The American Dream, *FAM and YAM* (New York: Coward McCann, 1961).

The Zoo Story and Other Plays (with *The Death of Bessie Smith*, *The Sandbox* and *The American Dream*) (London: Jonathan Cape, 1962).

Who's Afraid of Virginia Woolf? (New York: Atheneum, 1963; London: Jonathan Cape, 1964).

Tiny Alice (New York: Atheneum, 1965; London: Jonathan Cape, 1966).

A Delicate Balance (New York: Atheneum, 1966; London: Jonathan Cape, 1968).

Box and *Quotations from Chairman Mao* (New York: Atheneum, 1969; London: Jonathan Cape, 1970).

All Over (New York: Atheneum, 1971; London: Jonathan Cape, 1972).

Seascape (New York: Atheneum, 1975).

Counting the Ways and *Listening* (New York: Atheneum, 1977).

The Lady from Dubuque (New York: Atheneum, 1980).

ADAPTATIONS

The Ballad of the Sad Café (New York: Atheneum, 1963).
(Adaptation of Carson McCuller's novel.)

Malcolm (New York: Atheneum, 1965). (Adaptation of James
Purdy's novel.)

Everything in the Garden (New York Atheneum, 1967).
(Adaptation of Giles Cooper's play.)

Books on Edward Albee

R. E. Amacher, *Edward Albee* (New York: Twayne, 1969).

C. W. E. Bigsby, *Albee* (Edinburgh: Oliver and Boyd, 1969).

C. W. E. Bigsby (ed.), *Edward Albee: Twentieth Century Views*
(Englewood Cliffs, NJ: Prentice-Hall, 1975).

R. Cohn, *Edward Albee* (Minneapolis: University of Minnesota
Press, 1969).

G. Debusscher, *Edward Albee: Tradition and Renewal*, tr. A. D.
Williams (Brussels: American Studies Center, 1967).

R. Hayman, *Edward Albee* (London: Heinemann, 1971).

L. Kerjan, *Le Théâtre d'Edward Albee* (Paris: Klincksieck, 1978).

A. Paolucci, *From Tension to Tonic: The Plays of Edward Albee*
(Carbondale and Edwardsville: Southern Illinois University
Press, 1972).

M. E. Rutenberg, *Edward Albee: Playwright in Protest* (New
York: Avon Discuss Books, 1969).

A. M. Stenz, *Edward Albee: The Poet of Loss* (The Hague:
Mouton, 1978).

Index